# THE STORY OF

# BILL CLINTON
# AND AL GORE,
## OUR NATION'S LEADERS

## BY KATE McMULLAN

# A YEARLING BOOK

## ABOUT THIS BOOK

The events described in this book are true. They have been carefully researched and excerpted from authentic autobiographies, writings, and commentaries. No part of this biography has been fictionalized.

To learn more about President Bill Clinton and Vice President Al Gore, ask your librarian to recommend other fine books you might read.

Published by
Dell Publishing
a division of
Bantam Doubleday Dell Publishing Group, Inc.
666 Fifth Avenue
New York, New York 10103

Cover Photo Credit © Wesley Hitt/Gamma Liaison

The trademark Yearling® is registered in the U.S. Patent and Trademark Office.
The trademark Dell® is registered in the U.S. Patent and Trademark Office.

ISBN: 0-440-40843-1

Published by arrangement with Parachute Press, Inc.
Printed in the United States of America
January 1993
10  9  8  7  6  5  4  3  2  1
OPM

# Contents

To Jean Marzollo

# Preface

This is the story of Bill Clinton and Al Gore, the President and Vice President of the United States. Born within two years of each other, the two men grew up at the same time in America, but in some ways they were worlds apart. Bill Clinton's early days were spent in a small town in Arkansas, while Al Gore's home for most of the year was in the nation's capital and power center, Washington, D.C. How did history eventually bring these two men together?

Here you will read all about their lives and the very different paths they took to reach the White House. These are their stories as they unfold side by side, decade by decade.

# The Baby Boom

All over the United States, crowds gathered in the streets to cheer. It was 1945. World War II was over at last. Soldiers who had been fighting overseas were coming home. People celebrated and sang "God Bless America." Husbands and wives who had been apart would be together once more. Now they could start having families.

The next year, many babies were born in the United States—more babies than ever before in a single year. Everyone said it was a "baby boom." It was the start of a new generation.

One baby boy, William Jefferson Blythe IV, arrived on August 19, 1946. His mother, Virginia, must have felt happy to have a healthy new baby. But she must have felt sad, too, because her husband was not there to see his new son. On a rainy night three months before, he had been killed in a car accident.

Virginia and Billy, as the baby was called, lived in a small southern Arkansas town called Hope. Pine-tree woods surrounded the little town where everybody knew everybody else. Nearby farmers grew enormous watermelons. In fact, the town called itself the "Watermelon Capital" of the U.S.A.

Even though Billy did not have a father, he had aunts, uncles, cousins, and grandparents in Hope who loved him. For Billy, life in Hope was good. But Virginia worried about supporting herself and her son. She did not have enough education to get a good job, and there was no place in Hope where she could get the kind of training she needed. So the year Billy was three, Virginia left him with her parents, Eldridge and Edith Cassidy. Virginia went to New Orleans to go to school to become a nurse.

Billy's grandparents were happy to have their extremely bright little three-year-old grandson with them. When people came to visit, the Cassidys showed him off by having him read aloud from the newspaper.

At the time, Billy's grandfather worked as the night watchman at a sawmill. Some spring and summer nights, Eldridge Cassidy took his grandson to work with him. There Billy played on a mountain of pine-tree sawdust. When he got tired, his grandfather tucked him into the back seat of his car to go to sleep.

When Billy was four, his mother returned to Hope. She was a nurse now, a special kind, who helped give people anesthetics, or painkillers, when they had operations. Now she would always be able to find a well-paying job. Now she could work toward a better future for herself and her son. Virginia also was setting an important example for Billy. Hard work and persistence—sticking with something—pay off in the end.

That same year, Virginia married again. Roger

Clinton, who owned Hope's Buick dealership, became her second husband and Billy's stepfather. Virginia, Roger, and Billy moved into a house closer to the center of town, and Virginia took a job at the hospital.

Since both his parents worked, Billy often spent his days with his grandparents. They took him along with them when they went to work during the day in the small grocery store they owned just outside of Hope. Their little store looked very much like any other Arkansas grocery store in the early 1950s. But it was different from most others in one important way. It sold groceries to *all* of Hope's citizens, black people as well as white.

In the early 1950s, the state of Arkansas, like most states in the South, had *segregation* laws. This meant that black people and white people were supposed to stay apart. Black Americans had to go to different schools and churches from white Americans. Some drinking fountains and rest rooms had signs saying "White Only."

Because Billy's grandfather's store was not segregated, everyone was welcome. When customers came in to buy groceries, Mr. Cassidy showed all of them equal respect, no matter what color their skin. From him, Billy learned to do the same.

About this time, Billy started to learn about American presidents. His Grandfather Cassidy was a great fan of President Franklin D. Roosevelt, who had died in office the year before Billy was born. F.D.R., as the president was called, really cared about the people of the United States, Billy's grandfather told him. He was a great man.

While days at his grandparents' store were pleasant for Billy, nights at home were not. His stepfather was usually an easygoing man. He seemed to adore his new wife and stepson. But when he drank alcohol, Roger Clinton turned mean.

One night, when Billy was about four or five, Roger Clinton was yelling at Virginia. Billy saw his stepfather pick up a gun and fire a bullet right through a wall of the house. Billy ran from the room, and before long, the police came. They took Roger Clinton away, but after he sobered up, he came back. Billy had to live with him, and with that bullet hole in the wall. Every day, the sight of it reminded him of that unhappy night.

Billy wasn't the only one who knew about his stepfather's terrible temper. In a town as small as Hope, there were few secrets. With neighbors gossiping and relatives worrying, it was not an easy time for the Clinton family.

It was not an easy time for Roger Clinton at work either. His car business was doing poorly. Not many people in Hope could afford to buy a brand-new Buick. Roger and Virginia thought that maybe business would be better in a bigger town. Perhaps they thought that if they moved, their lives would be better as well. So Billy's family decided to leave the little town of Hope to make a new start.

~~~~~~

The "baby boom" was still going strong in 1948, when Albert Gore Jr. was born on March 31 in that year in Washington, D.C.

Albert Jr. had one older sister, Nancy. His mother,

Pauline, was a lawyer. His father, Albert Sr., was a well-known politician. The people from his home state of Tennessee had elected Albert Sr. to serve in the House of Representatives in Washington when he was only twenty-nine years old. There he helped to make the laws of our land. During most of the year, Albert Jr. and his family lived in a large apartment on the top floor of one of Washington's finest old hotels, the Fairfax. Albert Jr.'s family owned the whole hotel.

In 1952, when Albert Jr. was four years old, his father ran for an even more important office than the one he had. He asked the people of Tennessee to elect him to the Senate. They did. Tennessee voters were proud of this man who had represented them so well for so long.

Albert Jr. grew up surrounded by people who held powerful positions in government. When he played with toy submarines, it was at the U.S. Senate swimming pool. One time he even sat on Vice President Richard Nixon's lap while the vice president led a meeting of the Senate. His father liked to think that Albert Jr. was getting the best possible training for becoming a senator himself someday.

Each summer and during Senate vacations, the Gore family left Washington and returned to Tennessee. They lived on their farm just outside the little town of Carthage, which was not much bigger than Hope, Arkansas.

On the farm, Al, as Albert Jr. came to be known, learned how to groom cattle. Sometimes he would show a special cow at a country fair and win a blue ribbon. His time on the farm gave him the feeling that Tennessee was home.

Though Billy and Al both had been born during the "baby boom," their childhoods were very different. It hardly seemed likely that the two of them would ever meet. They did, however, have some important things in common. Both grew up watching their parents work hard toward a better future. And both grew up believing in the American Dream—that everyone in America is born with an equal chance in life, and that, with hard work and persistence, anyone can become whatever he or she dreams of being.

# New Hopes

Billy was seven years old when the Clinton family moved from Hope to Hot Springs, Arkansas, in 1953. Around Hot Springs, water bubbles up from fiery pockets deep within the Earth. The water rises quickly, before it has time to cool. The steamy water contains minerals, and many people believe that soaking in this mineral water will cure illnesses.

In the early 1950s, Hot Springs was known as a wild town. People traveled hundreds of miles to bathe in its waters. Many also loved to gamble in its famous casinos and visit its nightclubs. Another popular attraction was the racetrack.

At first, the Clintons lived in the country, outside of Hot Springs. Back then, living in the country in Arkansas meant that there were no sewer systems. The Clintons' house, like those of all their neighbors, had no indoor plumbing. Instead, there was an outhouse, or outdoor bathroom, in the back yard.

Each morning, Roger Clinton drove into Hot Springs to work as a service manager for his brother, who also owned a Buick dealership. Virginia worked in town as well. She had a steadier, better-paying nursing job than she'd had in Hope. Billy, too, traveled to Hot Springs every day, where he went to school. There he was known as Bill Clinton, although legally his last name was still Blythe. Since the Clintons spent so much of their time in Hot Springs, after a while they moved to a house in town.

Virginia Clinton took to Hot Springs right away. She was a free spirit who loved to go to the track and bet on the horses. Her husband, however, did not share her interest in horse races. He saw the racetrack only as a place where his wife could lose a lot of money. When Roger Clinton had been drinking too much and he suspected that Virginia had been to the track, he had fits of anger that led to terrible fights. But now the Clintons no longer lived in the little town of Hope, where everyone knew everyone else's business. In Hot Springs, they were able to keep their family problems to themselves.

Though the Clintons had some hard times, the family had many good times, too. And in 1956, when Bill was ten, Virginia gave birth to a second son, Roger Clinton Jr.

That same year, a presidential election was going on. While most other ten-year-olds watched Westerns on TV, Bill Clinton watched both the Democratic and Republican national conventions. He saw the Democrats nominate the brilliant Adlai Stevenson as their candidate, and the senior senator from Tennessee, Estes Kefauver, for the vice presidential spot. He saw the Republicans nominate the popular World War II hero, General Dwight D. Eisenhower, and his vice president, Richard Nixon, to run for a second term, which they won that fall. Each evening, after watching the conventions, Bill came to the dinner table and reported excitedly on what he had seen.

During his elementary school years, Bill was active in his church, school clubs, and the Boy Scouts. And his grades were straight A's, always. "The only bad mark he ever had in school was in conduct one time," his mother remembered later, "when the teacher decided to send him a message to stop trying to answer every question."

Bill entered high school in 1960, the year of another presidential race. In this one, a handsome, young Democratic candidate, John F. Kennedy, ran against the man who had been Eisenhower's vice president, Richard Nixon. In November, Americans elected John Kennedy. People hoped that under President Kennedy, the United States would become a better place to live. They compared what our country might become to Camelot, a legendary kingdom known for its peace and perfection. The nation's new leader made inspiring speeches. "Ask not what your country can do for you," President Kennedy said. "Ask what you can do for your country." All over the United States, people began to do things to serve their country.

Young Bill Clinton helped his country through community service with his church youth group and the Boy Scouts. Bill was also inspired to begin running for office himself. By this time, he had discovered his talent for organizing and managing things. He ran for office in every student organization he joined. One friend, Glenda Cooper, remembers their school days: "Bill was the kind of person who would come up to everyone new in high school and say, 'Hi. How are you? My name's Bill Clinton, and I'm running for something,' whatever it was. We always thought, well, someday Bill will be president."

Bill genuinely seemed to like talking to people about their ideas. And he was so good at managing things that he always won his elections. Finally, the high school principal had to make a rule that one student could hold only a certain number of offices. Otherwise, Bill would have held them all.

Bill presided over all his organizations very skillfully. He also continued to raise funds for charities, as well as be active in the Boy Scouts—and still make his usual straight A's. Some of his classmates remember Bill as being "disgustingly responsible." Yet because he was also outgoing, talkative, and cheerful, Bill had many friends. But neither his friends nor his teachers nor the pastor at his church knew about his difficult home life—not even his good friend and classmate Carolyn Staley, who lived right next door to him. Bill's troubled life at home continued to be a well-kept secret.

One night when Bill was fifteen, he heard his parents having a terrible fight in their bedroom. He was afraid that Roger was hurting Virginia. Bill had always hated his stepfather's ugly temper. Now, at last, he had grown big enough and brave enough to do something about it. Bill went to the door of his parents' bedroom, and, finding it locked, he broke it down. Virginia remembers that when Bill faced

Roger Clinton, he spoke in a quiet voice, calmly, but firmly, saying, "Don't ever lay your hand on my mother again."

Shortly after Bill stopped Roger Clinton from harming Virginia, his mother divorced her husband. With her sons, she moved into another house. But Roger begged Virginia to take him back. He promised to change, to quit drinking, to stop his ugly behavior. He told her to think of five-year-old Roger Jr. Desperately, Bill tried to keep his mother from listening to these pleas, but it was no use. In August of 1962, three months after their divorce, Virginia married Roger Clinton again.

Bill tried to make the best of things. He tried everything he could think of to help the family succeed this time around. He even changed his last name legally from Blythe to Clinton. But the family continued to have rough times. Years later, Bill Clinton said, ". . . I was the person who had to hold things together in my home, to keep the peace." Yet it was these difficult times that made Bill self-reliant and tougher than he might have been if his childhood had been less stormy.

Of course Bill did not spend all his time inside his troubled home or at school, leading committee meetings. Like any teenager, Bill and his friends also explored the town where they lived. And, in their case, it was a pretty exciting place. In Hot Springs, they saw the many tourists who came to gamble at the casinos and go to the nightclubs. Naturally, the boys tried out the slot machines themselves, and when they could, listened to the groups of musicians who were always

13

passing through town. It was in Hot Springs that Bill heard jazz for the first time—and he loved it. The musicians he admired most played jazz saxophone. Bill decided to take up the saxophone, too. He tried to play the way the jazz musicians did, and decided that someday, he would become a professional musician himself.

Bill began playing the saxophone in his high school marching band. In Arkansas at that time, people went wild over marching bands. Playing in a band at halftime during a football game was considered just as important as being a player on the football team itself. And Bill played the best saxophone in his high school band. He entered band contests, too. When he won, he got to travel to different towns in Arkansas and play in all-state bands. Bill became what was known in Arkansas as a "band boy."

During some summers of his high school years, Bill went away to band camp in Fayetteville, home of the University of Arkansas. There the camp director quickly learned that he could count on Bill to help him organize the many competitions that took place. Bill won first place in the state band's saxophone section. And he very much enjoyed playing in jazz groups.

During the summer of 1963, just before he began his last year of high school, Bill Clinton was deeply affected by two events. The first, he watched on TV. He saw Dr. Martin Luther King Jr., a leader of America's black people, standing before a crowd gathered at the foot of the Lincoln Memorial in Washington, D.C. There Dr. King delivered a most powerful speech. He said he dreamed that one day our country would live up to the American Dream. He dreamed that one day sons of people who had been slaves and sons of people who had owned slaves could be united in brotherhood. He dreamed of peace and equality for all Americans, no matter what color their skin.

Years later, Bill Clinton said, "I remember where I was when Martin Luther King gave that 'I have a dream' speech in 1963. I was home in Hot Springs, Arkansas, in a white reclining chair all by myself. I just wept like a baby all the way through it." Bill memorized every word of the speech. From that moment on, Dr. King joined President Kennedy as one of Bill's heroes.

The second important event of that summer of 1963 also took place in Washington, D.C. But this time, Bill did not have to watch it on television. He was there.

During his junior year in high school, Bill had been chosen to be one of a thousand teenagers from his state to attend a leadership training camp in Little Rock, the Arkansas capital. Like the others, Bill had been chosen because of his outstanding high school grades and activities. The camp was called Boys' State. There was also a Girls' State. These camps were sponsored by the American Legion. At the camps, model state governments were set up and campers ran for office. Bill ran for senator. He made fliers and passed them out. He shook hands with every Boys' State voter he could. And he gave a speech that sounded like one President Kennedy might have given. He spoke about the need for people all over the globe to get along with one another.

Bill won his election. At Girls' State, his friend Carolyn Staley also won hers. As a reward, they and the winning "senators" and "representatives" from other Boys' and Girls' States all over the country were given a trip to Washington, D.C. There they participated in model United States governments, called Boys' Nation and Girls' Nation. Then one warm July afternoon, they were escorted into the White House Rose Garden. All the young winners from all fifty states lined up to shake hands with President John F. Kennedy. The first one in line was Bill Clinton.

As soon as he got home from Washington, Bill gave his mother a photograph of himself shaking hands with President Kennedy. "I could just read the expression on his face," Virginia remembers, "and I never questioned what he was going to do."

# A Double Life

During the summertime, Al Gore Jr. was a country boy. With the children of farm workers, he played on the banks of the river that wound through his family's 500-acre Tennessee farm. He ran through fields with his collie, Buff, at his heels. Sometimes, he might drop a line into one of the farm ponds, hoping to catch a fish. Other times, he and his friends might try to see if what they'd heard was really true—that a chicken could be hypnotized by staring it right in the eyes.

From time to time, Al's parents had to be in Washington during the summer. Then Al would bunk with the farm manager and his family. In those days, living in the country in Tennessee, just as in Arkansas, meant no indoor plumbing.

During the day on the farm, Al always pitched in and helped with the chores. Sometimes he fed the chickens or mended fences. Other times, he groomed the cattle, shoveled manure, or helped with the hot, hard work of chopping tobacco, one of the crops on his father's farm. At night, he and his friends rounded up their dogs and went out hunting by the light of the moon. The farm manager's son, Gordon Thompson, who was just three years older than Al, remembers that Al ". . . just had a knack of fitting in."

But when fall arrived each year, Al's country life ended. That's when the family packed up and moved back into the apartment in Washington, D.C.

There, each morning, instead of feeding chickens or milking a cow, Al put on a freshly ironed shirt, tied his necktie, and put on a jacket. Dressed in this formal way, off he went to the St. Albans Episcopal School for Boys.

St. Albans, in an ancient stone building that looks as if it could be an English boarding school, is a very old and very fine school. Al and his friends who went there got an excellent education. Many of them would go on to attend the finest colleges. Even as young boys, they were being taught to take places of leadership in their country. And Albert Sr. made no secret of the fact that he was raising his son to hold political office someday.

Al seemed to thrive in a jacket and tie in Washington, D.C., just as he did running barefoot on the farm in Tennessee. He adapted easily to his double life.

But not everything was easy for young Al. When he was grown, someone asked his mother how he had liked being the son of a famous senator. She replied, "He *hated* it." Growing up with such a powerful and well-known father was hard for Al, partly because Albert Sr. stood up for his beliefs—and some of his beliefs were very unpopular.

Senator Gore represented Tennessee, a southern

18

state. In the early 1950s, most southern states' segregation laws said that black children and white children had to go to different schools. At the time, almost none of the white men who represented the South in Congress wanted to change these laws. Then in 1954, the justices of the U.S. Supreme Court, the highest court in our land, tried a case that tested the segregation laws. The Court declared that such laws were unfair, and ordered the all-white public schools to *de*segregate and let in black students.

Most people in the South, including their congressmen, did not like the Supreme Court in far-away Washington telling them what to do in their own states. In 1956, Senator Strom Thurmond from South Carolina drew up a document called the Southern Manifesto. It stated that segregation was a good idea for the South. He asked all the Southern congressmen to sign it, and most did.

Senator Gore was one of the few who did not. He believed that the Supreme Court was right. Desegregation was the only fair way to provide an equal education for all children.

Many Southern congressmen were very angry at Senator Gore. They called him a traitor. It must have been confusing for eight-year-old Al to hear such a thing said about his father, because other people admired Senator Gore for standing up for his beliefs. To them, he was a great hero. So much a hero that, at the 1956 Democratic Convention, he was one of the candidates nominated for vice president. Yet Senator Gore lost his party's nomination to run with Adlai Stevenson in November to the other senator from

Tennessee, Estes Kefauver. Once more, Al experienced the downside of politics.

But Al also must have observed that losing an election did not mean walking away from politics. Four years later, in 1960, the year Al turned twelve, another presidential election took place. Early in the year, Senator Gore hosted several important meetings at his family's apartment in the Fairfax Hotel. He brought together some of the most powerful Democrats in Congress to outline campaign plans for their party's candidate, John F. Kennedy. For the first time in eight years, the Democrats felt that they had a chance to win the election, but it was going to be a close race. Young Al, of course, was not invited to sit in on these strategy sessions. But that didn't stop him from hiding behind doors in the apartment and straining to hear what he could about the real inner workings of politics. And what better training could there be for someone who would one day hold office?

Al entered the high school at St. Albans in 1961. He was an honor student as well as a gifted artist. He played a fine game of basketball, won events for the track team, and in his senior year was football team captain. Popular and respected, he was also good-looking, with thick brown hair and dark eyes.

In 1964, the year before Al graduated from high school, his father again stood up for an unpopular cause. This time, Senator Gore went on record as being against U.S. involvement in the war in Vietnam.

South Vietnam and North Vietnam were two small countries in Asia. A group of revolutionaries, called the Viet Cong, was trying to overthrow the government of South Vietnam. The Viet Cong were being helped by North Vietnam and by the communist Soviet Union.

In World War II, the United States and the Soviet Union had been on the same side. But later, these two superpower countries became enemies in a time of bad relations known as the "cold war."

The Soviet Union had a communist system of government. Under this system, the government dictates what its people can or cannot do. The Soviet Union at that time wanted to spread communism all over the world. The United States wanted to remain a capitalist country, where its people had the right to control how they live and earn their money.

During the 1950s, both the Soviet Union and the United States built up huge supplies of weapons. Each country had the power to destroy the other. No one wanted a big war to start between these two countries.

But when the Soviets began helping the Viet Cong, some American leaders thought that the United States could fight communism by helping South Vietnam. In 1950, the U.S. Government quietly began sending military advisors and money to South Vietnam. Five years later, the United States began training the South Vietnamese Army. Every year, U.S. and Soviet involvement grew.

At first, most Americans believed that we should be helping South Vietnam. But a few, including Senator Gore, believed that the United States had no business there. Our country was not being threatened and should not get involved. In 1964, when Senator Gore spoke out against the war, many people claimed that he was un-American. They said he did not love his country.

From a young age, Al had observed how his father's career in politics had a double life of its own. One minute it was very rewarding, and the next minute it was very tough. Although he admired his father a great deal, Al came to have little desire to follow in his footsteps. As his high school days progressed, he was not sure what career he might choose. But he was sure of one thing: It would not be politics.

During his senior year in high school, Al went to a dance at St. Albans. There he met Mary Elizabeth Aitcheson, who attended a girls' school in Washington. Everyone called Mary Elizabeth "Tipper." Her mother had given her the nickname from a lullaby that was Mary Elizabeth's favorite when she was a baby.

Tipper had blond hair and sparkling blue eyes. She loved music and played the drums in an all-girl band called the Wildcats. From the night of that dance, Al and Tipper dated only each other.

In June of 1965, Al graduated from St. Albans. He had been accepted at Harvard University and planned to study English and become a writer. In the St. Albans' yearbook, a fellow student wrote about Al: "It probably won't be long before Al reaches the top. When he does, all of his classmates will remark to themselves, 'I knew that guy was going somewhere in life.' " (The same yearbook also mentions one of Al's less well-known talents. He was very good at lying on his back and balancing a broom on the tip of his nose!)

After his high school graduation, Al returned to Tennessee for the summer. One Saturday morning, his father recalls, Al asked his mother if he could invite his girlfriend to visit the farm.

"Sure," his mother replied. "When?"

Tipper arrived that same afternoon.

"She was the sweetest young lady you ever saw," Albert Sr. says. The next morning, she appeared, neatly dressed and perfectly groomed. "She came to the table," Albert Sr. recalls, "with her eye makeup exactly right, ready to go to a ball at breakfast. We fell in love with her. . . ."

Al had met Tipper in Washington, and now he had invited her to see the other side, the Tennessee side, of his life. Tipper Aitcheson was becoming a very important person in Al Gore's life.

# Troubled Times

In 1963, Bill Clinton had just started his senior year in high school when suddenly his world fell apart. On November 22, President Kennedy was shot and killed. The whole country mourned. Lyndon Johnson, who had been the vice president, was sworn in as president. But when President Kennedy died, so did the dream of Camelot. The nation entered a terribly troubled time.

Bill graduated from Lakeside High School in Hot Springs the following June. In the fall of 1964, he left Hot Springs to attend Georgetown University in Washington, D.C.

Washington must have seemed a very different place to Bill from the way it had been just a little more than a year before, when he had stood with the other eager teenagers from Boys' and Girls' Nation in the White House Rose Garden. Now large crowds of angry students came to Washington to demonstrate against the war in Vietnam. Other groups of students marched outside the White House to let President

Johnson know that our country's black citizens wanted the same rights as its white ones.

While in college, Bill worked as an intern for an Arkansas senator, William Fulbright. Bill admired Senator Fulbright a great deal and respected his strong position against the Vietnam War. Working in Senator Fulbright's office, Bill saw things that the demonstrators outside on the streets did not see, and these things made the far-away war seem much closer. Each day, a list arrived in the senator's office. On it were the names of young men from Arkansas who had been killed in Vietnam. Some of them were probably Bill's age. Or even younger. And they had died for a cause that millions of Americans believed was wrong.

In Bill's third year of college, 1967, he received some sad news from home. His stepfather was very ill with cancer. Roger Clinton lay dying in a hospital bed in Durham, North Carolina. As soon as Bill heard this, he drove from Washington to Durham to see Roger.

Every weekend that spring, Bill made the long, 265-mile drive. "I think he knew that I was coming down there just because I loved him," Bill remembered later. "There was nothing else to fight over, nothing else to run from. It was a wonderful time in my life, and I think in his." By the time Roger Clinton died, he and Bill had made their peace.

In 1968, during spring break of his senior year in college, Bill's good friend Carolyn Staley came to visit him. When she stepped off the plane in Washington, Bill met her with a grim face. Martin Luther King Jr.

had just been shot. The winner of the Nobel Peace Prize was dead. Now, angry people were rioting and setting fires throughout the country. Areas of Washington were in flames.

Bill told Carolyn, "We've got something to do." They drove to a relief center, where Bill got a large red cross and stuck it on the door of his white car. Then Bill and Carolyn loaded the car with medicine, blankets, and food. They drove into areas of Washington where the rioting was the worst. Buildings were burning as fires raged out of control. But the two friends managed to deliver their supplies to the neighborhood churches.

"It was very dangerous," Carolyn remembers. "We raced through red lights. But Bill just had to be there. He was devastated. Afterward, I remember him wandering around in a daze, muttering parts of King's 'I have a dream' speech under his breath, to himself."

Shortly before that, Robert Kennedy, the brother of the late president, decided to run for president himself. He had just won the primary election in California, when he, too, was shot and killed. Again, American cities were torn by rioting. Many people were killed. At the same time in Vietnam, American planes were dropping bombs. Many were dying there. It was a period of great sorrow and confusion in the United States.

When Bill graduated from Georgetown University in 1968, he received a great honor—a Rhodes Scholarship. The award gives scholars a chance to study for two years at England's famed Oxford University. Only a handful of the very brightest college graduates from the United States and England are asked to be Rhodes Scholars.

In the fall of 1968, just before Richard Nixon was elected president, Bill Clinton boarded the S.S. *United States* and set sail for England. He traveled across the Atlantic with the other American scholarship winners. But being among the brightest of their generation was not the only thing these young men had in common. All of them were also worried.

In those days, when a young man turned eighteen, he had to sign up for the draft, the government's system for selecting people for military service. If the young man passed a medical examination and was not in college, a committee called a draft board classified him 1-A. This meant that if our country needed soldiers, the young man would be drafted into the Army. As a soldier, he could be sent anywhere the Army wanted him to go. Even to Vietnam.

As college students, Bill and most of the young men aboard the S.S. *United States* had been safe from the draft. But a scholarship to Oxford did not count as college. Now Bill and many of his friends aboard that ship faced the draft, and faced the possibility of fighting in Vietnam.

Bill and his shipmates often talked late into the night. Most of them did not believe America should be fighting in Vietnam. If they were drafted, would they go into the Army? Or would they go to Canada and become draft resisters? Or would they say that they could not serve because they felt the war was wrong? What would they do? There were no easy answers.

But not all of Bill's time aboard the ship was spent thinking about such serious matters. With his wide smile and his down-home Arkansas friendliness, Bill soon knew almost everyone on the ship. When rough weather made many people seasick, Bill brought them chicken soup and crackers. On dull nights, he got out his saxophone and filled the big ship's ballroom with the mellow sounds of jazz.

Other nights, Bill joined conversations about career plans. He said that he hoped to go to Yale Law School. Then, he planned to go back to Arkansas, where he might run for senator or governor. "After that?" one friend asked, half-jokingly. And Bill admitted that maybe he'd run for President of the United States someday. Even in a group of unusually bright and ambitious young men, Bill Clinton stood out.

At Oxford, Bill studied government. He also played rugby and met his goal of reading a hundred books in six months. Then, in the spring of 1969, he got his draft notice.

The night after the dreaded letter arrived, several of Bill's close friends stayed up with him. They talked until dawn. By morning, Bill had made a decision. He would serve his country, but it would not be in Vietnam.

Bill decided to try to enroll in another kind of military program. One such program, for students, was called the Reserve Officers Training Corps, or ROTC. If Bill could get into a ROTC program, he would not be sent to Vietnam.

At that time, thousands of young men in Bill's position were looking for ways out of the draft. Many hoped to get into an ROTC program. Bill began writing letters, and he asked Senator Fulbright to help him. At last he was accepted into the ROTC program at the University of Arkansas. This meant he would have to enroll in the University's law school and give up his second year at Oxford. But he would not be drafted.

In the summer of 1969, Bill returned to Hot Springs. He stayed with his mother, who had married for a third time, and her new husband, Jeff Dwire, a hairdresser.

At home, Bill followed the news closely. Demonstrations against the Vietnam War were taking place all over the United States. Millions of protesters carried signs saying: U.S. GET OUT OF VIETNAM!

President Nixon had promised to stop drafting so many men into the Army. He began talking about a draft lottery. Under a lottery system, each day of the year would be assigned a number. If a young man's birthday fell on a day with a low number, he would be among the first to be drafted. If his birthday fell on a day with a high number, chances were good that the young man would not be drafted at all.

Bill wanted very much to go back for the second year of his Rhodes Scholarship at Oxford. And after that, as had always been his hope, he wanted to go to Yale Law School. Neither of these things would ever be possible if he enrolled in the University of Arkansas Law School.

Hoping for a high number in the draft lottery, Bill decided to take a chance. He did not withdraw entirely from the Arkansas ROTC program, but that fall of 1969, he went back to Oxford. He also sent a letter to his draft board asking to be reclassified 1-A again. Now all Bill could do was wait for the lottery. If he drew a high number, he would be free to continue his studies in England. If he drew a low number, he would return to Arkansas and enroll in the University's ROTC program.

Luck was with Bill. When the lottery numbers were picked that December, his birthday drew number 311 out of 365. That number was high enough. The very next day, Bill wrote and withdrew from the ROTC program. In the letter, he told about his antiwar feelings. "No government," he wrote, "should have the power to make its citizens fight and kill and die in a war they may oppose, a war which even possibly may be wrong, a war which, in any case, does not involve immediately the peace and freedom of the nation." That same day, Bill sent in his application for admission to Yale Law School.

Bill Clinton would not fight in a war he did not believe in. As it turned out, he did not serve his country in the military at all. Bill had gambled on his odds of being drafted, and he had won. Years afterward, many people would criticize him harshly for his actions. Yet in those confusing days of 1969, his choice must have seemed like the right thing for him to do.

# Another Choice

In 1965, Al Gore began his college career with a campaign. "The first time I met Al," a Harvard classmate recalls, "he came to my dorm room and said, 'I'm Al Gore, and I'm running for freshman council.'"

Al had planned to study English at Harvard. But he quickly changed his mind and switched his major to government. Yet at this point in his life, Al insisted that a career in politics was not for him.

The years that Al was at Harvard, from 1965 to 1969, were some of the most difficult in the nation's political history. Many American college students became carried away with antiwar activities. This peace movement, as it was called, sometimes turned violent. Students took over university buildings and kept classes from being held.

Al Gore believed the war in Vietnam was wrong, and he joined some antiwar demonstrations at Harvard. But he never became caught up, as so many students did, in protest after protest. "Al stood out to me," one of his Harvard professors remembers, "because he didn't get swept up in the . . . student movement. He had an independence of mind."

Yet in his own way, Al worked hard against the war. During the summer of 1968, he went back home to his family's farm, and became the chairman of Tennessee Youth for McCarthy. He then campaigned hard for Eugene McCarthy, the antiwar presidential candidate who was running against Richard Nixon.

While Al was at Harvard, Tipper studied psychology at nearby Boston University. She hoped someday to become a child psychologist. Like Al, she took part in student demonstrations against the war in Vietnam. The two continued to date throughout college.

In June of 1969, Al graduated with honors from Harvard. Once he was out of college, he went home to Tennessee, where he was classified 1-A by his draft board. And like Bill Clinton over in England, he wondered what he should do.

But Al's problems were different from Bill's. For one thing, in 1970, Albert Sr. would be up for reelection to the Senate. Although he had already served three terms as a senator from Tennessee, his upcoming election was going to be a tough one. The man running against him, William Brock, made many fiery speeches. He talked about Senator Gore's antiwar position. He said the senator was too liberal to represent Tennessee, and accused him of not loving his country. And voters were listening to what William Brock said.

Al's parents told him that they would support whatever decision he made about the draft. For a while, he thought about going to live in Canada. His mother even said that if he did do that, she would go with him. But his father's upcoming election worried Al. How would voters feel if Senator Gore's son fled to Canada to avoid the draft?

"It was a horrible time for all of us," Pauline Gore remembers. "And the pressure on young Al was enormous."

His father's upcoming election wasn't the only thing that bothered Al. Even though he had gone to school in Washington, Tennessee was his home. The little town of Carthage, where his draft board was, had a population of only 2,000 people at the time. Like every other American town, Carthage had a quota, or a certain number, of young men who had to go into the army each month. As Al said later, ". . . if you didn't go, it was no secret that one of your friends would have to go in your place. . . ." Although he believed the war was wrong, Al thought that if he were to go to Canada, he would be too ashamed ever to walk down Main Street in Carthage with his head up again.

After talking with his parents, Al went outside by himself and took a long walk beside the river where he had played so often as a boy. By the time he came back to the farmhouse, Al had made his choice. "I will go," he said. "I won't wait. I'll volunteer."

Al enlisted in the Army, and as soon as Tipper graduated from college in 1970, the two were married. Then Al reported to the Army for active duty.

That fall, Albert Sr. campaigned hard for his Senate seat. Voters knew he was against the war, but they also saw him in a campaign commercial with his only son in an Army uniform. In the ad, Senator Gore

33

reached out to touch Al's hand and said, "Son, always love your country."

But in November, Senator Gore lost the election to William Brock by a narrow margin. After serving in Congress for thirty-two years, Albert Gore Sr. retired from politics.

Meanwhile, Al was sent overseas after his basic training. Soon he was a part of the war he had protested. He served in Vietnam for six months. Stationed outside of Saigon as a reporter, he wrote articles for Army newspapers.

Al mailed some of his articles home to Tipper. She thought they were well written and gave them to an editor at a Nashville newspaper, *The Tennessean*. The paper published Al's pieces about Vietnam.

Al was one of the lucky soldiers. His job was a fairly safe one. He was not involved in active fighting. And he came home alive.

# Starting Out

**B**ill Clinton's final year at Oxford was a busy one. He studied hard, and became very involved in the peace movement. When the year was over, he returned to the United States.

In the fall of 1970, Bill arrived in New Haven, Connecticut. There he began his studies at Yale Law School. Like many young men at that time, Bill wore a beard and let his hair grow longer than it had been. Bill found studying law interesting, but not difficult. As he had in high school, he managed to make top grades and, at the same time, to become involved in many political activities.

In 1970, a candidate named Joe Duffey was running for the U.S. Senate from Connecticut. Joe Duffey firmly believed that the Vietnam War was wrong, and he promised to help stop it if he was elected. Quickly, Bill got involved in the Duffey campaign. He traveled around New Haven, talking to people, and he answered phones at campaign headquarters from sunup until late at night. He was well organized and worked hard. Many people were impressed. In the end, Joe Duffey lost the election. But he claimed victory in one district—the one where Bill Clinton had campaigned for him.

After the Duffey campaign was over, Bill had some catching up to do on his studying. He was in the law library one day having a conversation with a friend, when he noticed a young woman sitting across the room. Half-listening to his friend, Bill stared at the young woman. She seemed to be looking at him, too. After a while, she got up and walked over, then stood by Bill, waiting for him to finish his conversation. When he did, she said, "You know, if you're going to keep staring at me and I'm going to keep staring back, I think we at least should know each other. I'm Hillary Rodham. What's your name?"

This quick and to-the-point introduction surprised Bill Clinton. In fact, he was so surprised that, for a second, he couldn't even remember his name.

Hillary Rodham, a classmate of Bill's, had grown up in Park Ridge, a suburb of Chicago. Her father owned a textile company. Right from the start, Hillary liked to be the best at what she did. She earned every badge in the Girl Scout Handbook. She was elected president of her high school class. In her senior year, Hillary was so outstanding that her parents remember feeling slightly embarrassed as their daughter was called up to the podium time after time to accept various honors at her graduation ceremony.

During her teenage years, Hillary, like Bill, had heard President John Kennedy's call to serve their country. With the youth group at her Methodist church, she began volunteering in community service projects in some very poor sections of inner-city Chicago. Hillary organized things in her own neighborhood, too. Sometimes it was a circus. Other times, it was a field day. And always, it was for a good cause, such as earning money for migrant workers.

From high school, Hillary went on to Wellesley College, an excellent school for women. There she helped to organize the first Vietnam War protest. And as president of the student government, she made a speech her senior year. It was so good that *Life* magazine reprinted it.

Hillary was at the top of her class at Yale Law School. She was keenly interested in political activities and in discussing ideas. She didn't have much interest or time for things such as shopping for clothes.

Bill must have liked the straightforward manner of this serious young woman, for he remembers thinking, "Uh-oh, this woman is 'trouble'—the one I could love." After that first meeting in the law library, both Bill and Hillary knew that they had found someone special in each other.

With a group of other students, Bill and Hillary traveled to Texas during the summer of 1972. There Bill worked as coordinator for George McGovern's presidential campaign, while Hillary helped register voters. McGovern, a Democrat, was running against President Richard Nixon. If he was elected president, McGovern promised, he would stop the Vietnam War immediately.

The McGovern campaign was in full swing that fall when law school classes started again. But Bill and Hillary stayed down South and kept working. A fellow campaign worker, Betsy Wright, later recalled meeting the pair. "He and Hillary came down from Yale," she said. "I'd never been exposed to people like that before. I mean, they spent the whole semester in Texas, never attended a class—then went back to Yale and aced their finals. They were breathtaking."

In spite of the many idealistic young people working in his 1972 campaign, George McGovern lost the election to the Republican incumbent, Richard Nixon.

After graduation from law school, most of Bill's classmates hoped to get jobs with law firms. But not Bill. "All I wanted to do was go home," he said later. "I thought I would hang out my shingle in Hot Springs and see if I could run for office." As it turned out, Bill took a job in 1973 teaching law at the University of Arkansas.

Hillary, meanwhile, took a job in Washington—a job that Bill had turned down. She was serving as an attorney for the House of Representatives committee that would soon impeach, or bring charges against, President Nixon for engaging in illegal election activities.

Bill and Hillary stayed in close touch with long-distance phone calls. Bill kept asking Hillary to come to Arkansas for a visit. He wanted her to meet his family and see his state. But Hillary's job was very demanding. Finally, she arranged to take time off from work. She made a plane reservation and flew to Little Rock.

Bill met Hillary at the airport. On their way to Virginia and Jeff's house, he told her he'd like to show her some of the beauties of his beloved state. So Bill took the long way home. He showed Hillary scenic views from several Arkansas mountains, and he gave her a chance to sample delicious Arkansas fried pies. He wanted Hillary to fall in love—with Arkansas. The one-hour drive home from the airport stretched into nine hours.

When Hillary returned to Washington, she kept Bill informed about President Nixon's troubles. She was sure that he would not be president much longer.

Both Bill and Hillary thought that when voters learned of Nixon's illegal activities, they would distrust other politicians who had been his supporters. One of Nixon's strongest Republican supporters was Arkansas Congressman John Paul Hammerschmidt. In 1974, Hammerschmidt would be running for re-election.

As the 1974 election drew near, Bill decided that he would run for Congress against Hammerschmidt. Hillary returned to Arkansas to help Bill with the campaign. On election day, Bill lost—though not by very much. But he also had won something important. Now many people in the state of Arkansas knew the name Bill Clinton.

Bill's love for Arkansas must have rubbed off on Hillary. Before long, she, too, moved there. She settled into an apartment of her own in Fayetteville and began teaching at the law school.

During the next year, Hillary and Bill saw a lot of each other. Once, after Hillary had been away visiting friends, Bill again picked her up at the airport. She thought he would drive her to her apartment, but he headed in another direction instead.

39

At last Bill said, "I've bought that house you like."

Hillary said, "What house I like?"

"You know," said Bill. "Remember when we were driving around the day before you left, and there was a FOR SALE sign and you said, 'Gee, that's a nice house.'"

Hillary was surprised. "Bill, that's all I said. I've never been inside it."

"Well, I thought you liked it, so I bought it," he said. "So I guess we'll have to get married now."

A date was set. Dozens of Bill's friends helped him paint the little house by the lake. They had to rush to finish in time for the wedding because, through it all, Bill and Hillary were keeping up their busy teaching schedules.

Hillary's parents, Dorothy and Hugh Rodham, came to town for the big event. The evening before the wedding, Dorothy asked if she could see her daughter's wedding gown. No, she couldn't exactly. Still not much of a shopper, Hillary hadn't quite gotten around to buying one yet!

Dorothy rushed Hillary into town. It was late, and only one store was still open. When they went in, Hillary pulled a dress from the rack and bought it. The next day, she married Bill.

Hillary remembers a wonderfully slow-paced life in that little "surprise" house. She and Bill enjoyed having friends to dinner and talking with them for hours. Except for the sad death of Jeff Dwire, Virginia's third husband, from diabetes, it was a peaceful time for the Clintons.

But life did not remain slow-paced for long. Bill

and Hillary had been married in 1975. The next year, Bill ran for attorney general of Arkansas and won. Now he was in charge of all the legal affairs in the state. Bill worked hard. Among other things, he helped to keep people's electric and phone bills down. The citizens of Arkansas liked what he did. Two years later when he ran for governor of Arkansas, they voted him in. Bill and Hillary moved from their little house by the lake in Fayetteville into the governor's mansion in the state capital of Little Rock.

In 1978, at the age of 32, Bill Clinton had become the youngest governor in the United States.

When Al Gore got out of the Army in 1971, he returned to Nashville, where Tipper was living. *The Tennessean* offered him a job as a reporter. Tipper also worked for the paper, part-time, as a photographer.

At first, Al worked the night shift at the paper. As a beginning reporter, he got the assignments that no one else wanted. He investigated a pigeon-napping and wrote stories about dead cows. When Burger King sponsored an eating contest, cub reporter Al Gore was on the scene to cover it!

During the day, Al studied religion at Vanderbilt University. He was a Baptist, but he did not go to school to become a preacher. He went to study spiritual issues, which were important to him.

At *The Tennessean*, Al later graduated to police reporter, and then to covering politics. He investigated what was happening in the city government and he wrote about what he found. "He would spend hours combing through documents and reports, looking at

41

every possible clue and angle," recalls a reporter who worked with Al. A series of articles Al wrote in 1974 told how some city officials had taken illegal money, or bribes. Because of Al's articles, the officials were tried in court. Several of them were found guilty and sent to prison.

While covering the trials, Al became very interested in the legal system, so he enrolled in law school at Vanderbilt University in Nashville. This was a busy time for him. Besides studying law, Al became a home builder and a land developer. He also ran the farm where his family lived, raising cattle and tobacco. In 1973, with the birth of Karenna, Al and Tipper had also become parents.

Al continued working full-time for the paper, covering the city government, but now his work was less satisfying to him. "I felt intensely frustrated about policies and decisions I was writing about because I felt they were often dead wrong," Al remembers. "But as a journalist, I could do nothing to change them." Al began to wonder if writing about politics was really all that he wanted to do. A few of his close friends at the paper knew about his feelings.

One day in 1976, Al had just returned home from the paper. He was about to dash off to law school when one of his friends from the paper called with a hot tip: No one knew it yet, but the congressman in Al's district was going to retire. He would make his announcement in two days.

Al remembers, "I hung up the phone and told my wife, 'I'm going to run.' And I got down on the floor and started doing push-ups for the race."

Tennessee voters knew the Gore name from Albert Sr.'s years in Congress. Many also knew Al Jr.'s name from his newspaper reporting. But even with so much going for him, Al was nervous. He was so nervous that, right before he made the announcement that he was going to run, he had to excuse himself for a moment because he felt sick to his stomach.

Nevertheless, Al proved to be a good campaigner. And in 1976, he was elected to the House of Representatives. He was only 28 years old, a year younger than his own father had been when he was first elected to Congress. Just as his high school classmates had predicted, Al Gore was going someplace in life.

# Ups and Downs

College had been a snap for Bill Clinton. Law school had been a breeze. Running for office, organizing, and managing a campaign had all come naturally to him. But now he was the governor of Arkansas. And governing Arkansas, he found, was *not* easy.

Bill Clinton had plans for Arkansas. Big plans. Education specialists had ranked the state's schools the worst in the nation. They must be improved! The state's roads were in terrible condition. They must be fixed! He called in experts he had met at Yale and in Washington. He had work to do! He had things to accomplish!

But many people in Arkansas saw things differently. They saw a young governor with ambition. Maybe too much ambition. What was his big hurry to fix everything all of a sudden? And why had he brought in all those outside experts? Weren't Arkansas experts good enough for him?

Governor Clinton had a hard time getting money for all that he hoped to do. By law, the Arkansas governor's power to raise taxes was very weak. But Bill needed money to work with, so he raised fees on car license plates. Farmers now had to pay more for their license plates each time they sold a car or pick-up truck. They were not happy.

Many Arkansas people did not take well to Hillary either. They did not think it was proper for the first lady of Arkansas to continue her own work as a lawyer. Nor did they approve of her keeping Rodham as her last name.

But there were also joyous moments for the Clintons. On February 27, 1980, Bill and Hillary became the parents of a baby girl. Being fans of singer Joni Mitchell, Bill and Hillary had fond feelings for her song "Chelsea Morning," and they named their baby Chelsea. Bill was in the delivery room the night Chelsea was born. As he held his child in his arms, he thought about how this was a blessing that his own father, William Blythe, had never known.

That same year, Bill Clinton's two-year term as governor was up. Of course he ran again, but this time he lost. The Clintons moved out of the governor's mansion. The new governor, Frank White, moved in. At the age of 34, Bill Clinton became the youngest ex-governor in the history of the United States.

In 1980, Al Gore was serving his third term in the House of Representatives. One reason for his success was that he kept in close touch with the voters back home. When Congress was in session, he flew home to Tennessee nearly every weekend. There, he held open meetings. Everyone was invited to come and talk to him. The people of Tennessee felt they had someone in Washington who truly listened and understood how they felt about issues.

In Washington, Al became known for getting things done. He helped pass laws against selling worthless insurance. He helped set quality standards for baby formula sold in the United States. He became a leading expert on nuclear arms. He also led the campaign to put the sessions of the House and Senate on TV. He wanted the American people to be able to see what Congress was up to. Once people had looked up to Albert Gore Sr. Now they were starting to look up to his son in the same way.

By 1982, Al and Tipper were the parents of four children. When Karenna was three, Kristin was born. Less than two years later came Sarah. And when Sarah was three, Albert III arrived. Tipper's days as a free-lance photographer were over. She devoted herself to raising her four young children. And she was busy managing two households, one in Washington and one in Tennessee.

Al Gore served four terms in the House of Representatives. Then, like his father, he ran for the Senate. He was elected in 1984, when he was only thirty-six.

Yet as this happy event took place, a tragedy was unfolding in the Gore family. Nancy, Al's older sister, had been found to have lung cancer. The year Al was elected to the Senate, Nancy died from the disease. After his sister's death, Al stopped growing tobacco on his farm because of the connection between smoking and lung cancer. And in Congress he began working to pass a law requiring strong warning labels on cigarette packages.

~~~~~

Back in Arkansas, Bill Clinton was doing something that parents always tell their children is very important. He was learning from his mistakes.

Bill wanted to be Arkansas governor again. He knew he could do a good job. Trying to change the state overnight had not worked. Neither had bringing in experts from the East. The people of Arkansas were proud people. Well, Bill Clinton was from Arkansas, too. Now he just had to convince the voters that he was one of them.

Bill began campaigning. He went around the state and talked to voters. He shook their hands. Hillary went, too, but now she was called Hillary Clinton. She knew a great deal about education. She talked to the people of Arkansas about their children and about improving their schools.

Bill bought ad time on TV and apologized to Arkansas voters for raising the license plate fees. He was sorry, he said, that he had tried to do too much too fast. He'd made a young man's mistakes. But he'd changed. If they would elect him again, he would listen more carefully to the voice of the people. Next time, he would do things differently.

Governor Frank White campaigned hard against Clinton. He, too, went on TV. By his side was a leopard. He pointed to the leopard and reminded voters of the old saying: A leopard can't change its spots. And, he added, neither can Bill Clinton. If they elected Clinton again, White said, he would just raise taxes.

But Governor White had made some mistakes of his own. He had allowed gas and electric rates to go way up. And he had not fulfilled his campaign promise to bring more jobs to Arkansas. In November 1982, Bill Clinton defeated him. Now the Clinton family moved back into the governor's mansion.

And Bill Clinton meant to stay for a while. He rolled up his sleeves and got to work. But this time he did it differently. There was still not much money, but what there was, he put to good use. He set goals, and he concentrated on the most important ones. He became very good at getting a lot done for very little money.

For Governor Clinton, education was still the most pressing issue. He began a program of testing all students before they entered high school. He also began a program of testing teachers. And he raised their low salaries. He saw to it that schools all over the state taught basically the same things. He believed that parents must be involved in their children's education, so he required them to go to PTA meetings. If they missed a meeting, they were fined $50. He also said that students who dropped out of high school without a good reason would lose their driver's licenses.

Groups of Arkansas schoolchildren visited the Capitol Building in Little Rock each year. Governor Clinton always found time to talk with them, even if it meant keeping other people waiting a bit. Children mattered to Governor Clinton a great deal. And every time a schoolchild wrote to him, he made sure that the letter was answered.

Hillary helped her husband. According to a former secretary of education, she became one of the ten most knowledgeable people about education in the country. She also continued her own law practice. Twice in the late 1980s, she was rated one of the best 100 lawyers in the United States. She served on seventeen committees, including the board of the Children's Television Workshop, all the while continuing to be active in the Methodist Church. And she never missed one of Chelsea's softball games!

Bill and Hillary were a dynamic team. Leaders of the Democratic Party were beginning to notice them. They were beginning to wonder whether the hardworking governor of Arkansas might someday like to run for higher office.

Al and Tipper Gore were a dynamic team, too. Yet while Hillary often worked alongside her husband, Tipper worked for causes of her own.

One afternoon in the mid-1980s, Tipper and her children had gone to have lunch with Al in the Senate dining room. As Tipper was driving home, her daughters noticed a woman in ragged clothing standing on a street corner. The woman, Tipper told her daughters, was probably homeless.

"Can we help her?" the girls asked. "Can we take her home with us?"

They did not take the woman home, but Tipper decided to take action. She and her daughters began volunteering at shelters, and Tipper organized Families for the Homeless. "Every homeless person has one problem," says Tipper. "They don't have a home." The organization Tipper founded raises money to help homeless people.

Another afternoon, Tipper paused to listen to a rock song that her eleven-year-old daughter, Karenna, was playing. When she heard the song's words, Tipper was shocked. The song told about people killing themselves. It described other acts of cruelty and violence, too. And the song made these things sound perfectly all right. Tipper listened to more songs on her daughter's records and tapes. Many of them had the same kinds of lyrics. Tipper did not want Karenna listening to such songs.

Tipper contacted other congressmen's wives who had young children. She asked them to listen to several rock songs with words that told about sex and violence. The other mothers agreed with Tipper. They would not want their preteen children listening either.

Together, these women wrote to the Recording Industry Association of America. They asked that organization to develop a rating system for their records, tapes, and videos. The movie industry, they pointed out, had a rating system. The music industry should have one, too. Tipper and her committee thought that people buying music had a right to know if the lyrics were appropriate for young children.

Many newspapers and TV stations carried stories about Tipper's idea. In them, Tipper was made to look like a scolding housewife. She hates rock and roll, the stories said. She wants to ban it. She is for censorship! She doesn't want anyone to be able to listen to rock music!

None of this was true. Tipper only wanted a rating system. She wanted people to know what they were buying.

In 1985, Tipper's group arranged a hearing on record labeling before a Senate committee. There, senators questioned Tipper and the other women about their idea of a rating system for music.

After the hearing, reporters asked Tipper more questions. "Aren't you afraid that you are hurting your husband's career?" they asked. "I see this as my thing, not my husband's," Tipper answered. "I don't see this affecting my husband one way or another. I was an activist before I married my husband. I protested the Vietnam War and I worked for civil rights. This is not the wife of a senator who has suddenly gone nuts."

Tipper Gore wrote a book entitled *Raising PG Kids in an X-Rated Society*. She was against censorship. She felt that if people wanted to buy tapes with lyrics suggesting violence, they had a right to do so. She only wanted a rating system. But her activities put rock and roll on trial. Many people who were *for* censorship praised her. They used her cause to speak up for censorship. As a result, when some people heard the name Senator Al Gore, they connected it with censorship.

After all the hard work on many issues that Al had done in Congress, most of his mail now was about censorship. One 1986 letter said, "Dear Senator and Tipper: leave my rock and roll alone."

Tipper had tried to do something she believed was right. She had not expected the awful rumors and the

51

untrue stories. Yet without meaning to, she had affected her husband's career. This was no small thing. Many Democratic leaders were very interested in Al's career because they wanted him to run for president in 1988.

⚹⚹⚹⚹

At the same time in Arkansas, not everything was going smoothly for the Clinton family either. In 1983, Governor Clinton got a call from the state police. His brother, Roger, was in trouble.

The police told the governor that they had set up a sting operation. In it, a police officer disguised as a drug user tried to buy drugs. And he had bought some from Roger Clinton.

"What do you want us to do?" the state police officer asked the governor.

With a heavy heart, Bill answered, "Do what you'd normally do."

Bill knew that the police would continue the sting operation for a few more weeks. An undercover police officer would keep trying to buy drugs from his brother. And, with a secret camera, Roger would be filmed selling the drugs. When the police had plenty of evidence against Roger, they would arrest him. Then they would try to find out who was supplying him with drugs.

For six weeks, Governor Clinton kept the sting operation a secret from everyone but his wife. "I never knew whether my brother or my mother would forgive me," Governor Clinton said later. "It was a nightmare. But it was the right thing to do."

When the sting operation finally ended, Roger

Clinton was arrested. He went to jail for a year and a half. The police told Governor Clinton that his brother's drug habit had been very serious. If he had not been in such good physical shape, they said, it would have killed him. In jail, Roger had to stop using drugs. When he got out of jail, Roger, Virginia, and Bill met for family counseling sessions. At first, Roger felt betrayed by his brother. Then he realized that Bill had saved his life by making him face his problems before it was too late.

Following his recovery, Roger is reported to have stayed off drugs. He lives in Los Angeles, where he works as a production assistant on a TV show.

After the episode with Roger's drug problem, nothing else happened to rock Bill Clinton's governorship. He served the 1986-87 term as chairman of the National Governors' Association. This meant that he often traveled around the country. Governor Clinton met with other governors and powerful politicians everywhere. It was a fine chance for him to find out how they would feel about a new campaign: Bill Clinton for president in 1988.

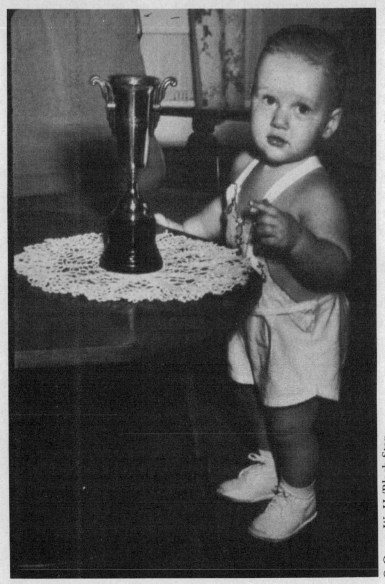

*As a 1-year-old baby in Hope, Arkansas, Bill Clinton is known as William Jefferson Blythe IV, or Billy.*

*Billy as an 8-year-old in 1954.*

*Bill Clinton remembers meeting President John F. Kennedy during the summer of 1963 in Washington, D.C., as a high point of his life.*

*Bill poses for the camera before his high school graduation in 1963.*

*From left to right, Roger Clinton (Bill's brother), Virginia Kelley (Bill's mother) holding baby Chelsea Clinton (Bill's daughter), and Bill Clinton himself.*

*Bill, Chelsea, and Hillary enjoy a family dinner at the governor's mansion in Little Rock, Arkansas.*

*Arkansas Governor Bill Clinton runs through the streets of Little Rock on October 3, 1991—the same day he reveals his decision to run for president.*

*Bill plays the saxophone on the campaign trail in New Hampshire, November, 1991.*

*Albert Jr. as a 4-year-old in July, 1952, with his parents and 14-year-old sister, Nancy, on vacation.*

*Tennessee Senator Albert Gore Sr. and his wife say good night to their 8-year-old son Albert Jr. as they leave for a formal White House reception.*

© Sygma

*Al Gore Jr. and Elizabeth "Tipper" Aitcheson marry in 1970.*

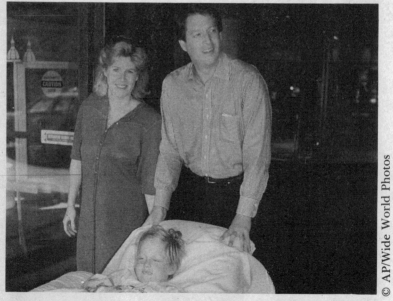

© AP/Wide World Photos

*Six-year-old Albert Gore III leaves the Johns Hopkins Hospital in Baltimore with his parents on April 26, 1989, after a miraculous recovery from a car accident.*

*Albert Gore Jr., Bill Clinton's running mate, poses in this 1986 Christmas photo with his family—his wife, Tipper, his son, Albert III, and his three daughters, Sarah, Karenna, and Kristin (second row—left to right).*

*A moment of triumph for Hillary, Bill, and Chelsea at the Democratic National Convention in New York City, July 1992.*

# The 1988 Primary

**P**oliticians. News reporters. Democratic voters. They all had their eyes on Bill Clinton and on Al Gore. Here were two bright, handsome, hardworking young men. Surely they would be running in the 1988 Democratic presidential primary elections.

In a presidential primary, candidates from the same political party run against one another. The winner becomes the party's candidate in the general election for President of the United States.

Primary elections are held state by state. When voters in each state vote in a primary, they are really electing delegates to represent them at their party's big convention. There the delegates nominate the presidential candidate from their party. States with large populations, such as California, elect many delegates. States with small populations, such as North Dakota, elect only a few delegates.

Bill Clinton knew just how tough running in a primary race could be. Candidates must travel all over the country. They begin this a full year before the first primary. They give speeches and shake hands with thousands of voters. That leaves little time for anything else.

In the summer of 1987, Bill Clinton made a surprising announcement. He would not run in the next Democratic primary. He would not seek the Democratic nomination for president.

Bill Clinton had a state to govern. But that wasn't the only thing that stopped him. Chelsea was just seven years old. She was in school. She would not be able to travel all over the United States with her father. If he ran, Bill Clinton would not get to see much of his daughter for a year. He remembered his own childhood. He wanted to give his daughter something he had not had—a caring father. In his announcement, Governor Clinton stated that a primary campaign might be too hard on seven-year-old Chelsea. But he gave the strong impression that Chelsea would probably be able to handle a campaigning father better by 1992.

That same summer of 1987, Al Gore announced that he would be running in the primaries. He became the final and the youngest of seven Democratic candidates.

Al Gore was well known in Washington, D.C., in Tennessee, and in the states that surrounded it. But many people in other areas of the country did not know who he was. So Senator Gore hit the road. He traveled the country, giving intelligent speeches. He was an expert on arms control. He had served in Vietnam. He was religious. He was handsome. And he had a good family name. These things appealed to voters. In fact, one reporter said that Al Gore seemed "too good to be true."

But he was criticized, too. Al Gore is too wooden, some reporters wrote, and it is hard to listen to his stiff speeches. They went on to say that he didn't really have many good ideas about what he would do if he was elected. The press began saying that none of the Democratic candidates had any good ideas. News writers nicknamed them "The Seven Dwarfs."

In the course of the campaign, some people accused Al of supporting censorship. But not all voters felt that Tipper's run-in with the music industry had been so bad. Sometimes when Al arrived at a campaign rally, fans would hand him Tipper's book to autograph. Other voters carried signs with slogans such as "Grandmas for Tipper."

In the early spring of 1988, the primary elections began. Senator Gore did very well in the South. He was riding high until he arrived in New York. There he made a big mistake. The mayor of New York City, Ed Koch, was feuding with Jesse Jackson, an African-American political leader who was also running in the primaries. Reporters accused Senator Gore of trying to be friends with Mayor Koch, who was Jewish, to get New York's Jewish people to vote for him. Other reporters said that Al Gore did not care about Jesse Jackson and New York's African-American people. The conflict made Senator Gore look foolish. Two days after the New York primary, he withdrew from the race. The winner of the primaries turned out to be the governor of Massachusetts, Michael Dukakis.

But now voters throughout the country knew the

name Al Gore. Even though some people thought he had given rather formal speeches, others liked what they had heard. Senator Gore hoped that he would be a stronger candidate in the next set of presidential primaries in 1992.

In June of 1988, the Democratic National Convention was held in Atlanta, Georgia. Delegates from all fifty states gathered to nominate Michael Dukakis for president. The honor of giving the nominating speech went to none other than Bill Clinton.

Governor Clinton worked hard on his speech, practicing it over and over. He had a lot to say. Maybe the speech would run a bit long, but he believed that all of it was important.

On the third night of the convention, the time arrived for Governor Clinton's nominating speech. He stepped up to the podium and began addressing the thousands of delegates. He spoke about what an outstanding president Michael Dukakis would make. Everyone cheered. He talked about how something had to be done in this country about the lack of concern for our children. Many people cheered. But as he talked on and on and on, the cheering faded. After about fifteen minutes, the TV cameras cut away from Bill Clinton's face to a flashing red light near the podium. The light meant "stop talking!" But Bill Clinton ignored the light. The cameras went on to film delegates looking bored. Then some in the audience began chanting, "Get off! Get off!" No one cheered at all.

Governor Clinton went on for more than thirty minutes. At last he said, "In closing, . . ." *Now* the delegates cheered! When he finished, Bill Clinton left the podium. He had just given one of the worst-received speeches in U.S. history.

A political advisor, Samuel Berger, was backstage during the speech. He said, "Had I been Bill at that point, I would have gone out and dug the deepest hole I could and buried myself."

But Bill Clinton did not dig himself a hole. Instead, he marched from the stage straight into the press room. He knew he would face hostile questions from reporters. He knew it would be embarrassing. But he went anyway. "Instead of running away from the problem, he faced it," said Mr. Berger. "He took responsibility."

Political cartoons in newspapers all over the country poked fun at Bill Clinton's long speech. People joked about it. They made quips such as, "I heard he wrote eight drafts of the speech; he must have forgotten to throw away the first seven."

Bill Clinton took the jokes in stride. He did not let the criticism stop him. As he had in the past, he would learn from his mistakes. In the future, he would work harder on his talks. After all, he knew a powerful speech when he heard one. Dr. King's "I have a dream" speech had meant a great deal to him when he was younger. He would have to work to make his own speeches better—especially if he was going to realize his dream.

After the convention, Bill Clinton returned to Arkansas. He continued the excellent job he had been doing as governor. The state's schools were improving. People became proud of the progress their state was making. Before long, the governors of all fifty states would take their yearly vote to decide which governor had been the most effective. The winner would be Governor Bill Clinton of Arkansas.

That November, Michael Dukakis lost the election for president. The Republican candidate, George Bush, won by a landslide. For a while, the Democrats retreated. They didn't say much about who they would nominate for president the next time around.

But as the next presidential election year approached, many Democratic party leaders looked again at Bill Clinton. They listened to what he was saying and found him to be very impressive. Maybe he'd learned something from his 1988 nominating speech. Maybe he'd be ready for bigger things in 1992.

# Real Problems

It seemed a sure bet: Bill Clinton and Al Gore would run against each other in the next Democratic presidential primary. Both of them were ambitious. Both were smart. Both were after the number one spot on the ticket. It would be a tough race.

Over the years, Governor Clinton and Senator Gore had met each other. After all, Arkansas and Tennessee are neighboring states. And both men had been active in Democratic politics for many years. Yet they had had very little to do with each other. Perhaps they knew that someday they would go head-to-head for the nomination.

By the spring of 1989, Senator Gore was already preparing for another exhausting primary race, even though he was not in the best of spirits. After a life of success, the flop of his 1988 campaign had stung him. But Senator Gore was determined. This time around, he thought he would do better.

Then a terrible thing happened.

Baseball season had just opened, and Senator Gore had taken his six-year-old son, Albert, to a Baltimore

Orioles game. After the event, they left Memorial Stadium and walked toward their car. Suddenly, Albert pulled his hand away from his father's. He dashed across the street and into the path of a speeding car. The car struck Albert, throwing the little boy thirty feet into the air, then dragging him along the pavement for another twenty feet. Senator Gore rushed to Albert's side. He held his son, calling his name, but Albert did not answer. He was limp in his father's arms. He was not breathing and had no pulse. His unblinking eyes were empty. Al Gore was experiencing the worst nightmare a parent can have. He knelt in the gutter, holding his son, and prayed.

Albert was rushed to the hospital in an ambulance. He was still unconscious and terribly injured. One leg and several ribs were broken, and his internal organs had been crushed. Albert would have to fight hard for his life.

For a month, Albert barely clung to life. He had several operations. Both his parents stayed constantly at his bedside. And then, ever so slowly, he began to get better.

Little Albert went through a lot of pain, but he was very brave. A family friend remembers that he once said to his parents, "I can't get well without you."

That was all Al needed to hear. He dropped out of the primary race. It was far more important for him to be with Albert than to be out campaigning.

Sitting endless hours beside his son's hospital bed, Al did some serious thinking. He thought about what mattered in life. Senator Gore thought of the most important thing he could do for his son, for his daughters, and for every other child on our planet. He decided he would put his energy into protecting the environment. Right there in the hospital room, Al Gore began writing a book on how we must take care of our world. The book is called *Earth in the Balance*. Al wrote it because he wanted our planet Earth to be as lovely as possible when it was time for the next generation to inherit it.

Finally Albert was able to leave the hospital and go home. Every morning, his parents helped him exercise his legs. Every evening, they prayed with him. His three sisters helped him, too. And when at last he started teasing them again, everyone knew he was feeling better. After nearly a year, Albert was up and running. He had recovered completely.

It is often very hard for parents to recover from a child's close brush with death. Al especially had feelings that, somehow, he should have been able to keep the accident from happening. People at the hospital told the Gores that other parents in their situation had been helped by family counseling, and so the Gores went. And they were helped, too. Tipper later said, "I think because of the time that we spent together, we've become much stronger as a family."

Together, Al and Tipper agreed that Al would not try to get back into the race. Al Gore would not be running for president in 1992.

But Bill Clinton was ready to run.

In the fall of 1991, Chelsea Clinton entered the seventh grade. All the Clintons agreed that now she was old enough to cope with her father being away a lot of the time and her mother not being around as much as usual. Hillary planned to take a leave of absence from her law firm so that she could help her husband campaign.

Besides, Chelsea now had a busy life of her own. She was an excellent student with many good friends. She played on her school's volleyball team, and on the Molar Rollers softball team, sponsored by a local dentist. But her real love was ballet. She had already danced in Little Rock productions of *The Nutcracker.* And plans for the summer, when the campaign would be in full swing, included a few weeks at a foreign-language camp in Minnesota and then a ballet camp. Like many busy preteens, Chelsea probably wouldn't spend too much time with her parents even if they were at home!

Even so, Bill wanted Chelsea's opinion, so he asked her if she thought he ought to run. "It's going to be tough," her father told her. "They'll say terrible things about me."

Chelsea answered, "Dad, they always say terrible things about you. You ought to go to my school. You can't imagine the things they say. You've just got to blow it off and go on."

Clearly, Chelsea was tough enough to take whatever the primary elections might bring.

Governor Clinton had never run in a primary race before. Although powerful Democrats knew him, he was not widely known. And four other candidates were running against him. He needed to make voters outside of Arkansas familiar with his name and his record as governor.

Yet sometimes, when he first hit the campaign trail, Bill Clinton did run into people who had heard of him. A newspaper editor from South Carolina knew his name. "Aren't you the guy," the editor asked, "who gave that awful speech for Dukakis at the 1988 Democratic Convention?"

"You want to hear the rest of it?" Bill Clinton joked. "Go get yourself another cup of coffee."

Unlike many politicians, Bill Clinton turned out to have a sense of humor. Not only that, but he seemed genuinely friendly. And he had a talent for politics. "I like people, and like to help them," he once told a reporter. "I can get them together, organize them, help them reach their goals."

Perhaps Bill Clinton had learned to make his speeches shorter, but he still liked to talk. Reporters who followed his campaign got used to it. When they asked him a question, Bill was sure to have an answer. A *long* answer. But Bill Clinton wasn't just giving them prepared lectures. Each of his answers was full of good ideas. And he actually seemed to be enjoying himself.

The winter before the spring primary elections began, newspaper articles began appearing, naming Bill Clinton as the favorite Democratic candidate. The Democrats had lost five out of the last six presidential elections. They really needed a candidate who could beat the Republican incumbent, George Bush. Bill Clinton had run in eighteen different elections in the past seventeen years. He'd lost only two. He looked like someone who could win against Bush.

Governor Clinton had a plan for health care. He

had a plan for creating new jobs. And one for education. Bill Clinton became known as "a man with a plan."

This was a time when many people had lost their jobs or were in danger of losing them. For most families, money was tight. A poll taken that spring of 1992 found that three out of every four people in the country thought that "America was off on the wrong track." The things Bill Clinton said sounded pretty good. Maybe he was the one to help America get back on the right track.

News stories also compared Bill Clinton to another young presidential candidate. He looks a bit like John F. Kennedy, they said, and he has the same spirit. He is in his early forties, just as Kennedy was when he ran for president.

The first presidential primary is always held in New Hampshire. The whole country watches to see what the voters in that small state do. And the voters there take their responsibility very seriously. Many times, voters in other states follow New Hampshire's lead.

A few weeks before the New Hampshire primary, things looked good for Bill Clinton. But then the situation began to change for the worse. Reporters asked him where he had been during the Vietnam War. Had he been drafted or not? Had he been in ROTC? What exactly *was* his military record? And when he answered their questions, his reply wasn't very clear. Something wasn't making sense to the voters of New Hampshire.

People who had lost sons or husbands or brothers in the war did not like Bill Clinton's answers. Maybe the

Vietnam War had been a terrible war. Maybe America never should have gotten into it in the first place. But their loved ones had gone to fight anyway. They had not figured out a clever way to avoid the draft.

Then matters got even worse. Some reporters found a copy of the letter Bill Clinton had written in 1969 to the ROTC officer in Arkansas. Six days before the New Hampshire primary, part of the letter was printed in a newspaper article. It said: "Thank you . . . for saving me from the draft." Governor Clinton's campaign manager took one look at the article and said, "We're dead."

But another campaign advisor read the entire letter. He told Governor Clinton to release the whole letter to the press. He did. And other parts of it showed Clinton's deep feelings about the war. It showed the struggle he had gone through to make his decision. Many who read the entire letter felt that he had made an honest choice for those times.

A few days later, a military leader, David Hackworth, who had been in Vietnam in 1969, wrote a letter about Bill Clinton to *Newsweek* magazine. In it he said, "If he had been eager to go to Vietnam as a 23-year-old student in 1969, I would question his credentials as presidential material in 1992." The article reminded people that in 1969, some of the protests against the war had been led by Vietnam veterans themselves. They had thrown their military medals into the gutter.

Reporters stopped asking Governor Clinton about the draft.

But Bill Clinton hardly had time to catch his breath

before another ugly story appeared. Bill Clinton, the story said, had a secret girlfriend. Bill and Hillary, it went on to say, had a terrible marriage.

The paper that printed this story was the kind that people buy at supermarket checkout counters. Such papers are not respected news sources. They often print gossip and shocking stories about movie stars and other famous people. Some of their stories turn out to be true. Others do not. Also, real newspapers do not pay people to tell their stories. But this paper had paid the woman in the story a large sum of money to say what she said about Bill Clinton.

Governor Clinton denied that the woman was a secret girlfriend. But rumors started flying, and Bill and Hillary had to deal with them. They accepted an invitation to appear on TV's popular *60 Minutes* program. There they talked about their sixteen-year marriage. No, they admitted, it hadn't always been perfect. It had gone through some rough times, as many marriages do. But they had worked hard to make their marriage better. Now they were closer than ever.

But even after this explanation, many New Hampshire voters were not so sure about Bill Clinton any more. They felt some of his answers had not been totally honest. Maybe he could talk intelligently about many issues, they thought, but he seemed to have a way of saying whatever people wanted to hear. Sometimes it appeared as if he simply wanted everyone to like him—and vote for him. But what did he really care about? People weren't sure. The press nicknamed him "Slick Willie."

But Bill Clinton was more determined than ever for people to know who he really was. To get his message across, he traveled around New Hampshire. He made speeches. He met the people. He shook their hands. Reporters stopped calling him "Slick Willie." When the voters of New Hampshire went to the polls on February 18, Bill Clinton came in second to Paul Tsongas. It wasn't the prized first place, but it was a respectable finish.

Throughout the New Hampshire campaign, voters had seen Bill Clinton under fire. He had responded very well. People began to think that maybe the negative things said about him were being overstated. Now it was Bill Clinton's turn to give himself a nickname. He was, he said, "The Comeback Kid."

# The Comeback Kid

**B**ill Clinton had certainly picked the right nickname for himself. After the New Hampshire vote, he was back in the race. But he had more troubles ahead, and before the primary race was over, he would need his sense of humor.

Two days after the New Hampshire primary, on February 20, a new figure appeared on the political scene. It was Texas billionaire Ross Perot. Perot was a guest on the *Live with Larry King* TV show. He said that he would run for president, but he would not run as a Republican—or a Democrat. He would run as an independent, a candidate of the people, as he put it. And he would run only if people got his name on the ballot in all fifty states.

Many frustrated American voters listened to Ross Perot. They were sick of the old political parties. Whichever one was in power, not much seemed to happen. Maybe an independent candidate was a good idea. And Ross Perot was certainly a business whiz. He had started his own company and turned it into a billion-dollar operation. Maybe he was just what America needed.

Perot supporters got busy. They set up booths in shopping malls and along highways. They knocked on doors. They asked people to sign their names to a petition that said Perot should be allowed to be on their state ballots. Many people signed. But— at that point, anyway—few people believed he could be much of a candidate without a political party behind him.

A more direct problem for Bill Clinton was an attack on Hillary. Another Democratic candidate, Jerry Brown, said that her law firm did business with the state of Arkansas, and that Hillary Clinton made money from such business. He said that she should not be a lawyer in Little Rock while her husband was governor.

"I suppose I could have stayed home and baked cookies and had teas," Hillary replied. "But what I decided to do was fulfill my profession."

Reporters jumped on this quote. The next morning, it was in every newspaper. Mothers all over America who had chosen to stay home to raise their children felt insulted.

Hillary tried to explain. She had only meant that she could have served as a hostess for Bill in the governor's mansion, but she had chosen, instead, to practice law. She had, she said, great respect for women who stayed home to raise their families.

But now reporters began to examine other parts of Hillary Clinton's career. Some looked into her work for the Children's Defense Fund. They read complicated legal opinions she had written. They took down a sentence from one page and another sentence from another page. But apart from the whole article, the sentences did not make sense. That did not stop reporters from printing the separate sentences in newspapers, however. Hillary Clinton, they said, thought it was all right for children to sue their parents. And furthermore, they said, Hillary Clinton had written that the institution of marriage was like slavery. Hillary responded to these twisted statements as best she could, and many legal scholars came to her defense. Still, many people believed what they had read in the papers.

Meanwhile, the Clinton campaign headed to Georgia and South Carolina. Down South, the press kept right after Bill Clinton. One minute, things looked up. The governor's husky southern accent and his comic imitation of Elvis Presley, the King of Rock and Roll, singing his hit song, "Don't Be Cruel," earned him an affectionate new nickname: Elvis.

But the next minute, another negative story would hit the papers. And Governor Clinton would have to defend himself again. One newspaper said Bill Clinton was ". . . like some kind of Robo-candidate, full of bullet holes but still plowing ahead. . . ."

Even without reading damaging half-truths about himself in the paper each morning, Bill found the campaign trail difficult. He made so many speeches that at one point he lost his voice. He fought off colds. Too often, dinner was rubbery chicken and tasteless vegetables in a plastic container held on his lap in the car on the way to the next speech.

But in spite of everything, Governor Clinton won

in the South. Now he geared up for Super Tuesday. On that day, March 10, eleven states had primary elections. Among them were states with many delegates—Texas, Massachusetts, Missouri, and Florida. Bill Clinton tried to be everywhere at once. And after the vote was in, he looked better than ever.

In the Midwest, too, Clinton ran well—so well that his strongest opponent, Paul Tsongas, pulled out of the race. Things looked very promising for the governor as he traveled to New York.

New York is known as a tough town. Four years before, it had destroyed Al Gore's campaign. Bill Clinton must have wondered how the Big Apple would treat the candidate from the "Watermelon Capital" of the United States. Not well, it seemed at first. City papers ran huge headlines, questioning Clinton's character.

Clinton's campaign managers had arranged many meetings for their candidate in New York, but he canceled them all. Instead, he went out to the city streets. He walked around, talking to people. He shook their hands.

Bill also agreed to be interviewed by Don Imus, a famous New York City radio personality known for saying wild things on the air. On his show, Don began by asking Bill, "Did you ever finish that speech at that '88 convention?"

"That's why I want to be the nominee for president," Mr. Clinton quipped. He added that if he became his party's candidate, he could talk as long as he wanted. "I've got about thirty more minutes to finish that speech in Atlanta."

New Yorkers appreciated his humor. And by a small margin, he won the state's primary.

By now, Bill Clinton had won hundreds of state delegates. At the convention in July, they would vote for him. It was beginning to look as if he would be the Democratic candidate for president.

The primary campaign had been going on for months now. Hillary tried to return home to Little Rock every three or four days to be with Chelsea. Bill did not get back as often. But when Chelsea had a ballet recital, her father always made sure he was in the audience.

When Bill was away, he missed his daughter very much. And it worried him that she had seen some of the negative things about him in the news. When he and Hillary asked Chelsea what she thought about these reports, she answered, "I think I'm glad that you're my parents."

Now a new problem cropped up. It wasn't another negative news story. Bill Clinton was getting used to handling those. The problem was that there weren't enough stories about him. Or about George Bush. Someone else was making all the news: Ross Perot.

Back in February, when Ross Perot first announced that he was willing to run for president, no one had taken him very seriously. But in state after state, people were signing the petitions to put him on the ballot. Perot support was growing stronger each day.

By June, it became clear that Bill Clinton was going to be the Democratic nominee for president. George Bush would be the Republican choice. That month, a poll was taken, asking voters whom they were going to vote for. One out of every three people answered, "Ross Perot." It looked as if it was going to be a tough three-way race.

Even though he had the Democratic nomination sewn up, Bill Clinton kept going. He, too, appeared on TV programs. He played his saxophone on *The Arsenio Hall Show* and was interviewed on MTV. He tried to reach new audiences that might not tune into a political show. Bill Clinton didn't quit campaigning until the last primary was over.

Occasionally, Republicans seemed to be helping him out. Like Bill Clinton, Vice President Dan Quayle went out to meet the people. One day, he went to an elementary school in New Jersey. There he coached 12-year-old William Figueroa in a spelling bee. And when William got the word "potato," the vice president incorrectly told him to spell it with an *e* at the end. Every newspaper in the country picked up the story, and many people used it to make jokes about Dan Quayle and the Republicans. Some people quipped that his poor spelling was proof that voters should elect the Democrats. After all, the critics said, Republicans can't even spell *potato*—that must mean it's time for a change.

Soon the Democrats had to get ready for their big convention. They needed to come up with a platform—a program to tell voters all over America what they stood for and what changes they proposed in order to make America a better place to live.

And it was time for Bill Clinton to name a running mate. He began with a list of forty names. Usually, a candidate chooses a running mate who is very different from him or her in important ways. When young John Kennedy from the northern state of Massachusetts ran for president, for example, he chose an older running mate, Lyndon Johnson, from the southern state of Texas. In that way, candidates try to get votes from different sections of the country and from people of different ages.

Bill Clinton quickly narrowed the list to six people. Senator Al Gore was among them. But not many people thought that Clinton would pick Gore. The two were very much alike. Both were "baby boomers." Both were from the South and had gone to the best schools in the East. They even shared the same religion, Baptist. Besides, everyone knew that Al Gore did not want the number two spot. Once he had even said that being vice president was a "dead end." Surely Bill Clinton would have to pick someone else.

During the late spring, Governor Clinton talked several times with each of his six preliminary choices. An aide remembers, "Every time Bill would come away from a conversation with Gore and say, 'He's so smart.' " Finally, after a long meeting with his advisors, Bill Clinton made up his mind. "I think I'm ready," he announced. "I'm going to ask Senator Gore to run."

A few years earlier, Al Gore would not have accepted. He'd had his eye on the ticket's top spot. But things had changed. Now he saw that he *could* help his country by serving as its vice president. It was, in many ways, a powerful position. It would help him to be even more effective in his work to save the Earth's resources. And so Senator Gore said yes.

Bill Clinton and Al Gore had many things in common, but they also had differences that would help them. Bill Clinton's career had been in Middle America. Al Gore's had been in Washington. Bill Clinton, as governor of a state, keenly understood how he could help people in America. Al Gore had more experience dealing with foreign countries and arms control. And Al Gore was a Vietnam veteran. Even Tipper was a valuable asset to the ticket. With the Republicans saying they were the only ones who understood the importance of family values, Tipper Gore's ideas about a rating system for rock and roll lyrics were suddenly seen in a new light. It turned out she'd been ahead of her time in taking real family values to heart.

The last primary election was in early June in California. When it was over, Bill and Hillary went home. It was the first real time off they'd had together in eight long, hard months of campaigning. Chelsea was very excited to be at home with her parents again. They couldn't wait to do all the things they had missed doing together for so long, such as playing cards with Hillary's parents and visiting with Virginia and her fourth husband, Richard Kelley.

The next time Bill Clinton would be in the spotlight would be at the Democratic National Convention.

# Time for a Change

**Sunday, July 12, 1992**

Convention eve. The Democratic party had rented Madison Square Garden at a cost of $4 million. Secret Servicemen searched the huge space. Their job was to make sure that it was safe for the big event.

Delegates and alternates from every state had been arriving in New York City all week. Monday evening, all 4,928 of them—plus 5,000 of their family members and closest friends, plus 380 important people from 87 foreign countries, plus 13,500 reporters—would pour through the doors of Madison Square Garden. Twenty-five hundred New York City police officers had been assigned to crowd-control duty in the area. After months of preparation, the Democratic Convention was about to begin.

**Monday, July 13, 1992**

By 5:00 P.M., Madison Square Garden was packed with Democrats who were ready to cheer and whoop and holler. Up on the ceiling, a net held 60,000 balloons that would be released at just the right moment of celebration. Everyone was ready to have a good time and get the Democrats off to a great start for the fall elections. *This* was a political party.

Many people were dressed in red, white, and blue, or in stars and stripes. Many of them held up signs: *Illinois Loves Bill Clinton* or *Good-bye, Mr. Bush.* Some people wore outrageous hats. One had a model of the White House on it and a sign saying: *Future Home of Bill Clinton.* A delegate from Washington State wore a button that read: *Hillary's Husband for President.*

William Figueroa, the boy Dan Quayle had prompted incorrectly in spelling *potato,* had been invited to the convention. One evening, he would lead the delegates in the Pledge of Allegiance.

At last people settled down—a bit. Opera star Marilyn Horne sang "The Star-Spangled Banner." New York Mayor David Dinkins welcomed everyone to the city. Five Democratic women who would be running for the Senate in the fall spoke. It was, they said, time for a change. Michael Dukakis, the last Democratic presidential candidate, declared that "Bill Clinton is the Republicans' worst nightmare." Other speakers said that George Bush did not care about the American people; that Ross Perot talked big, but had no plan; that in a three-way race, Bill Clinton could beat them both. Every time the names *Bill Clinton* and *Al Gore* were mentioned, everybody cheered and waved their flags. The Democratic Convention was underway.

**Tuesday, July 14, 1992**

To open the second night of the convention, Aretha Franklin belted out "The Star-Spangled Banner." Then two people who have AIDS spoke. They told of their struggle with this terrible disease and of how the government needed to budget money for AIDS research. By the time they were finished speaking, many people were crying. Later, former President Jimmy Carter spoke. So did African-American leader Jesse Jackson. Other speakers told of how the Democratic platform put people first. Everyone agreed: It was time for a change.

**Wednesday, July 15, 1992**

On this night, the Boys' Choir of Harlem sang "The Star-Spangled Banner." Senator Edward Kennedy introduced a film about his brother, Robert Kennedy, and he talked about his other brother, John Kennedy. The names of these great fallen leaders reminded everyone of the hope of former days—of Camelot. Maybe now there was reason to hope again.

Later, New York Governor Mario Cuomo stood at the podium to nominate the Democratic candidate for president. He gave a powerful speech, finishing with these challenging words: "So step aside, Mr. Bush. You've had your parade. It's time for change—someone smart enough to know, strong enough to do, sure enough to lead. The Comeback Kid. A new voice for a new America."

Then, one by one, the states cast their delegate votes. They voted by roll-call, in alphabetical order. After the Arizona delegate sat down, Virginia Kelley stood up. "Madam Secretary," she said, "Arkansas proudly casts our forty-eight votes for our favorite son and my son, Bill Clinton."

While the states voted, the Clintons watched the convention on a TV in a restaurant in Macy's Department Store. They saw the "great state of Ohio" cast its 144 votes. That's when Bill Clinton knew he had enough votes to clinch the nomination. At Madison Square Garden, confetti began showering down from the ceiling. The Democrats had their man.

Bill Clinton hugged Chelsea and Hillary. He was wearing a blue suit. Hillary wore red. Chelsea was dressed in white. Then, as 22 million Americans watched on their TVs, the patriotic trio began walking the block and a half to Madison Square Garden. Supporters along the way cheered and waved CLINTON signs. Inside Madison Square Garden, Bill and Hillary's families greeted them. Bill's brother, Roger, had tears of happiness shining on his cheeks.

**Thursday, July 16, 1992**

Early in the morning, before the convention opened, Bill Clinton was working on his acceptance speech. It would be the grand finale of the convention. Suddenly, a news story broke. Ross Perot had dropped out of the race. He would not be running for president! Quickly, Bill Clinton made some changes in his speech.

That night, Al Gore was nominated for vice president. He began his acceptance speech by saying, "I've been dreaming of this moment since I was a kid growing up in Tennessee: that one day, I'd have the chance to come here to Madison Square Garden and be the warm-up act for Elvis." The crowd roared. After the laughter died down, Al Gore told of how proud he had always been of his father, who had worked for civil rights and for ordinary people. He told about his son's terrible accident and how it had helped him realize that we are all a part of something much larger than ourselves.

But as Al Gore then said, this night belonged to Bill Clinton. As Governor Clinton made his way to the podium, a video presented scenes from his life. It showed him at the age of sixteen, shaking hands with President Kennedy. It showed him at home with Hillary and Chelsea.

Then a hush fell over Madison Square Garden. Bill Clinton stood behind the podium. At six feet two inches, with his beginning-to-gray hair, square jaw, and piercing blue eyes, he looked quite presidential. Bill Clinton talked about his grandfather and his mother, who, he said, had taught him to keep fighting. He spoke to "every child who is trying to grow up without a father or mother," adding then, "I know how you feel." He told them not to let anyone tell them they couldn't be anything they wanted to be. He spoke to the people who had supported Ross Perot and been so greatly disappointed by his withdrawal from the race. He said he understood how much they wanted the government to change. "Join us," he said, "and together we will revitalize America." And when he concluded his speech, referring to his birthplace, he said, "I end tonight where it all began for me: I still believe in a place called Hope."

The applause of thousands and thousands of people echoed in Bill Clinton's ears. The convention had come to an end. But the race was just beginning.

# Bill and Al

After the convention, Bill Clinton and Al Gore's popularity soared in the polls. They didn't want to let up now. So the candidates, their wives, some campaign staffers, reporters, and several Secret Service agents boarded eight buses. They began a 1,000-mile tour through eight states, from New York to Missouri.

Most candidates travel by jet. But the Clintons and Gores wanted to take the back roads. They wanted to shake hands with Americans everywhere. Some of their stops along the way had been planned, but not all of them had. When it looked as if a good-size crowd of people had gathered at the roadside, the buses pulled over. And Bill and Al and Hillary and Tipper got out to meet the people.

In Pennsylvania, one man waited for two hours to see the candidates. His four-year-old son was sleeping on his shoulder. "I have a young family," the man told a reporter afterward. "I believe Clinton's the one who's going to look out for us."

Bill Clinton thrived on meeting the people. *All* the

people. At one stop, he was greeted by an Elvis impersonator. At another, a man asked him what kind of saxophone he played. But most people just wanted to see what the candidates and their wives were really like, to touch them, to feel a connection with them. And to tell them that they agreed: It *was* time for a change.

After the first bus tour, there was a second. The buses headed north along the Mississippi River, from Missouri to Minnesota. The candidates visited fast-food restaurants and talked to the workers there. At an aluminum-siding plant in Davenport, Iowa, someone gave the candidates hard hats to wear. The hats had big letters spelling out their names: Bill and Al.

Trip followed trip, but not everything went smoothly. Once, the Gore staff bus broke down. Sometimes the handshaking took place in the pouring rain. Bill Clinton is a night person. Getting on the road at 6:00 A.M. wasn't always easy for him. Neither was talking to reporters at that hour—and making sense. Al Gore, on the other hand, normally likes to get to bed at 10:00 P.M. But many times the buses didn't pull into the last stop until the wee hours of the morning. Along the way, all the campaigners learned the one thing they could always count on: Expect the unexpected.

In Minnesota, Tipper Gore was shaking hands with voters who were lined up to meet her. She noticed that two people down the line had some kind of animals with leashes around their necks perched on their shoulders. When she got closer, she saw that the animals were large white rats. One of the owners held a rat out to Tipper and asked if she wouldn't like to pet it.

"Don't worry," the man said. "She won't bite."

Tipper petted the rat. She even held her for a little while before handing her back to her owner. Then she moved on to shake hands with the next people in line. Everyone who saw her do this will remember Tipper Gore as a plucky campaigner.

While the Clinton-Gore buses were traveling through America's heartland, people in Washington, D.C., were eating cookies. Hillary's remark about "staying home and baking cookies" had become famous. A baking company asked her if she had a recipe for chocolate chip cookies. She did indeed. The company also asked President Bush's wife, Barbara, for her cookie recipe. The company then baked both recipes and sold the cookies to some restaurants in the nation's capital. There, diners could sample the unmarked cookies and vote on which tasted best.

The cookie competition between Democrats and Republicans was friendly. But not everything else was. Sometimes the Republicans struck out at the Democratic candidates. They said that Bill and Al were too much alike. They said that they would ruin the economy—that they were too young to run the country. Again, they brought up the Vietnam issue and made Hillary's work for children's rights seem as if she were out to destroy the American family.

But as Bill Clinton had said to voters earlier, "I'll be there for you until the last dog dies." And he meant it. The Clintons and Gores kept going. The bus trips were exhausting. Yet there were so many moments that more than made up for all the late nights away from home and all the cold rubber-chicken dinners.

When Martha Duerson, the mother of eleven children, approached Bill Clinton, she said, "My great-grandmother was a slave and she told me about the day she saw President Lincoln. Now I can say to my grandchildren that I saw President Clinton before he became president."

# Election '92

All summer, Bill Clinton and Al Gore kept their lead in the polls. Even the Republican convention in August did not give President Bush's popularity much of a boost, so the Democrats kept their lead during September.

But on October 1, Governor Clinton and President Bush got a surprise. Billionaire businessman Ross Perot announced that he was back in the race. His supporters had put his name on the ballot in all fifty states. Perot had promised that if they did this, he would run for president. Once again it was a three-way race.

In mid-October, the candidates debated one another on television. Governor Clinton talked about what changes he would make to help the country. President Bush talked about how his Democratic rival would make a poor president. Little that they said sounded new. But Ross Perot sounded different. He did not talk like a politician. He made fixing big problems in the United States seem simple. After the first debate, almost half the people watching thought that Ross Perot had done the best job.

Yet the polls showed that most people still intended to vote for Bill Clinton. So once more President Bush began to attack his opponent. He said that Bill Clinton was wrong to avoid the draft. He criticized Bill Clinton for demonstrating against the Vietnam War while he was a student in England. He said that Bill Clinton could not be trusted. In the polls, President Bush's popularity began to rise. Just a week before the election, a few polls showed that President Bush and Governor Clinton were almost tied.

Bill Clinton kept up his strong campaign. He talked about his ideas for creating new jobs. He talked about how he would help the economy. He talked so much about his many plans that he grew hoarse. One night he lost his voice completely, and Hillary had to finish his speech for him.

As Election Day neared, the polls showed that the race was going to be close. So Bill Clinton stopped taking bus trips and boarded a jet. On the day before the election, he flew over 4,000 miles, landing in nine states to bring his message to the people.

On November 3, Election Day, all across America voters turned out in record numbers. In parts of North Dakota and Minnesota voters braved snow to get to the polls. In Georgia some people stood in the hot sun for two hours before getting their turn inside a voting booth. In rainy New York City, one elderly man waiting at the end of a long line said, "I just hope I live long enough to vote!"

On election night, television news programs showed a map of the United States. As the votes were tallied, a state on the map would turn red for a Republican electoral victory and blue for a Democratic win. Hour by hour the map turned bluer and bluer. And when Ohio's votes were counted, Bill Clinton's electoral votes exceeded the 270 he needed (out of 538) to become forty-second president of the United States.

Because so many people had voted for Ross Perot, Bill Clinton received less than fifty percent of the popular vote. But Bill Clinton had won the election.

It was nearly midnight in Arkansas when the Clinton and Gore families appeared outside the Old State Capitol in Little Rock. This was the moment Bill Clinton had been dreaming of since that long-ago day when he met President John F. Kennedy in the White House Rose Garden. As Al Gore said later, this election changed more than leaders. It changed generations. For the first time, our country's leaders would be people born after World War II.

In a husky yet strong voice, President-elect Clinton addressed the cheering crowd: "My fellow Americans, on this day with high hopes and brave hearts, in massive numbers, the American people have voted to make a new beginning." In the spirit of President Kennedy, he asked Americans to be interested not just in getting but in giving. "Together we can make the country that we love everything it was meant to be."

With these words, William Jefferson Blythe Clinton, the man from Hope, began a new era of leadership in the United States of America.

# Glossary

**campaign**—A plan for winning an election. Bill Clinton shook hands with voters as part of his *campaign*.

**candidate**—A person who wants to be voted into office. Bill Clinton was a *candidate* for president.

**capitalism**—A system in which land, factories, and other means of producing goods are owned and controlled by individual people instead of the government. The economy of the United States is based on *capitalism*.

**censorship**—The act of keeping out of the public's reach something that someone has judged to be objectionable. Banning certain books from a library is a form of *censorship*.

**civil rights**—The rights of every citizen of a country, such as the right to vote, to live anywhere, and to have equal protection under the law. In the 1960s, black people had to fight to gain their *civil rights*.

**cold war**—A state of tension between two countries that stops short of actual armed combat. The United

States and the Soviet Union were enemies in a *cold war* that lasted for forty years.

**communism**—A system in which land, factories, and other means of producing goods are owned and controlled by the government and are supposed to be shared by all people equally. For many years, the government of the Soviet Union was based on *communism*.

**Congress**—The branch of the U.S. government that makes laws. The U.S. *Congress* is made up of people elected to the House of Representatives and to the Senate.

**conservative**—A person who favors things staying the way they are and is cautious about change. Many *conservatives* believe that the government should have as small a role as possible in people's lives.

**Constitution**—The document containing the law and plan of government for the United States. It is the president's job to make sure that people are getting the rights they are guaranteed by our *Constitution*.

**delegate**—A person who is chosen to act for others. At the Democratic National Convention, most *delegates* cast their votes for Bill Clinton.

**Democrat**—A person who belongs to the Democratic party, one of the two major political parties in the United States. Bill Clinton is a *Democrat*.

**desegregate**—To do away with the system of having separate schools and other facilities for people of different races. The Supreme Court ordered all-white schools to *desegregate*.

**draft**—The selecting of persons for military service. Young men had to register for the *draft* when they turned eighteen.

98

**economy**—The management of a country's money and resources. When the *economy* is good, many people have jobs.

**House of Representatives**—The lower house of Congress, chosen according to a state's population. States with small populations elect fewer people to the *House of Representatives* than states with large populations.

**impeach**—To bring formal charges of wrongdoing against a public official. The U.S. House of Representatives voted to *impeach* President Richard Nixon.

**incumbent**—A person currently holding a certain office. George Bush was the *incumbent* in the 1992 presidential race.

**liberal**—A person favoring change and progress as ways of improving things. Many *liberals* believe that the government should play an active part in people's lives.

**nominate**—To choose as a candidate. Political parties *nominate* candidates for president.

**nominee**—A person who is nominated. Bill Clinton was the Democratic *nominee* for president.

**petition**—A formal request made to a person in authority. People who wanted Ross Perot's name on the ballot in their states asked voters to sign a *petition* making that request.

**platform**—A statement of principles or beliefs of a group. A political party's *platform* is announced at its convention.

**policy**—A guiding belief or plan that people use to help them make decisions. The way a government responds to another country is called its foreign *policy*.

**political convention**—A meeting of delegates elected

in each of the fifty states to nominate a presidential candidate from their political party. The Democratic National Convention and the Republican National Convention are *political conventions*.

**poll**—A collecting of opinions. A *poll* showed that Bill Clinton was ahead of George Bush in the presidential race.

**polling place**—The location where votes are cast. Americans go to a *polling place* to vote for president every four years.

**primary**—An election in which members of the same political party run against one another to determine who will be the party's candidate. During the New Hampshire *primary*, Bill Clinton had strong competition from several other Democrats.

**representative**—One who is elected to speak or vote for others; a member of the House of Representatives. Because California has a large population, it elects many *representatives* to the House of Representatives.

**Republican**—A person who belongs to the Republican party, one of the two major political parties in the United States. *Republicans* are usually considered more conservative than Democrats.

**segregate**—To keep one race of people separate from another. Senator Al Gore Sr. knew it was unfair to *segregate* black children in separate schools from white children.

**Senate**—The upper house in Congress. Each of the fifty states elects two members to the U.S. *Senate*.

**senator**—A member of the Senate. Al Gore served as a *senator* from the state of Tennessee.

**U.S. Supreme Court**—The highest court in the United States. In 1954, the *U.S. Supreme Court* ordered the desegregation of public schools.

**unconstitutional**—Not in keeping with the U.S. Constitution, and therefore, against the law. Not allowing a person to take a job because of his or her race is *unconstitutional.*

*Highlights in the Lives of*

# Bill Clinton and Al Gore

**1946**  Bill Clinton is born on August 19.

**1948**  Al Gore is born on March 31.
Harry Truman, a Democrat, is elected president.

**1949**  Virginia Blythe goes to New Orleans to train as a nurse.

**1950**  Virginia Blythe returns to Hope, Arkansas, and marries Roger Clinton.
The United States sends military advisors and money to South Vietnam.

**1952**  Al Gore Sr. is elected to the U.S. Senate.
Dwight Eisenhower, a Republican, is elected president.

**1953**  Bill Clinton's family moves to Hot Springs, Arkansas.
The Korean War ends.

**1954**  The U.S. Supreme Court outlaws school segregation.

**1955** The United States begins training the South Vietnamese Army.

**1956** Senator Al Gore Sr. refuses to sign the Southern Manifesto.
Dwight Eisenhower is reelected president.

**1960** Bill Clinton enters high school in Hot Springs.
John Kennedy, a Democrat, is elected president.
Many demonstrations for civil rights for blacks occur throughout the United States, and continue through the '60s.

**1962** Virginia divorces Roger Clinton, then remarries him.

**1963** Bill Clinton attends Boys' Nation and shakes hands with President Kennedy.
Martin Luther King Jr. gives his "I have a dream" speech and leads a march on Washington.
The first demonstration against U.S. involvement in Vietnam is held.
President Kennedy is assassinated.
Vice President Lyndon Johnson succeeds to the presidency.

**1964** Bill Clinton enters Georgetown University.
Al Gore meets Tipper Aitcheson at a school dance.
Lyndon Johnson is elected president.
Martin Luther King Jr. receives the Nobel Peace Prize.

**1965** Al Gore graduates from St. Albans School and enrolls in Harvard University.

**1967** Roger Clinton Sr. dies of cancer.
In New York City, 200,000 people march to protest the war in Vietnam.

**1968** Al Gore coordinates Eugene McCarthy's antiwar presidential campaign in Tennessee.
Martin Luther King Jr. is assassinated.
Bill Clinton delivers food to riot-torn areas of Washington, D.C.
Robert Kennedy is assassinated.
Bill Clinton graduates from Georgetown University and goes to England as a Rhodes Scholar.
Richard Nixon, a Republican, is elected president.

**1969** Al Gore graduates from Harvard.
Bill Clinton receives a draft notice.
Two million people nationwide demonstrate against the war in Vietnam.

**1970** Bill Clinton enrolls in Yale Law School.
Bill Clinton meets Hillary Rodham.
Al Gore marries Tipper Aitcheson and reports for active duty in the Army.
Senator Al Gore Sr. loses his election for the Senate.

**1971** Al Gore joins the staff of *The Tennessean* in Nashville.

**1972** Bill Clinton and Hillary Rodham go to Texas

to work on George McGovern's antiwar presidential campaign.

Al Gore studies religion at Vanderbilt University.

Richard Nixon is reelected.

1973 Bill Clinton takes a teaching job at the University of Arkansas Law School.

A peace treaty is signed, ending the Vietnam War.

Karenna Gore is born.

1974 Bill Clinton runs for Congress and loses.

Hillary Rodham moves to Arkansas.

Al Gore enrolls in Vanderbilt University Law School.

Under heavy pressure, President Nixon resigns.

Vice President Gerald Ford succeeds to the presidency.

1975 Bill Clinton and Hillary Rodham are married.

1976 Al Gore graduates from law school and is elected to the House of Representatives.

Bill Clinton is elected Arkansas attorney general.

Jimmy Carter, a Democrat, is elected president.

1977 Kristin Gore is born.

President Carter pardons 10,000 draft resisters.

1978 Bill Clinton is elected governor of Arkansas.

1979 Sarah Gore is born.

**1980** Bill Clinton is defeated for governor of Arkansas.
Chelsea Clinton is born.
Ronald Reagan, a Republican, is elected president.

**1982** Bill Clinton is reelected governor of Arkansas and remains in that office until 1993.
Albert Gore III is born.

**1983** Roger Clinton Jr. is arrested for selling drugs and goes to jail.

**1984** Al Gore is elected to the Senate.
Ronald Reagan is reelected.

**1985** Senate hearings take place on developing a voluntary rating system for the Recording Industry Association of America.

**1986** Tipper Gore's book, *Raising PG Kids in an X-Rated Society,* is published.

**1988** Al Gore runs in the Democratic presidential primaries.
Bill Clinton delivers the nomination speech at the Democratic National Convention.
George Bush, a Republican, is elected president.

**1989** Albert Gore III is hit by a car and is critically injured.

**1991** Al Gore's book, *Earth in the Balance,* is published.

**1992** Bill Clinton endures a tough primary race and gives himself the nickname "The Comeback Kid."

Bill Clinton is nominated for president at the Democratic National Convention. Al Gore is nominated for vice president.

On November 3, Bill Clinton is elected president, and Al Gore, vice president.